IMAGES
of America

LAKE TAHOE'S
WEST SHORE

ON THE COVER: The full image from the cover appears above. The passenger steamer SS *Tahoe* launched at Glenbrook in 1896 and is moored at the Tahoe City railroad pier. She is shown alongside the narrow gauge locomotive No. 1 Glenbrook as she takes on passengers c. 1910. The Tahoe Tavern hotel is in the background. (E.F. Mueller Postcard Collection, California History Room, California State Library, Sacramento, California.)

IMAGES
of America

LAKE TAHOE'S
WEST SHORE

Carol A. Jensen
North Lake Tahoe Historical Society

ARCADIA
PUBLISHING

Published by Arcadia Publishing
Charleston, South Carolina

Library of Congress Control Number: 2011934316

For all general information, please contact Arcadia Publishing:
Telephone 843-853-2070
Fax 843-853-0044
E-mail sales@arcadiapublishing.com
For customer service and orders:
Toll-Free 1-888-313-2665

Visit us on the Internet at www.arcadiapublishing.com

482 Sweetwater Drive
1986–2008

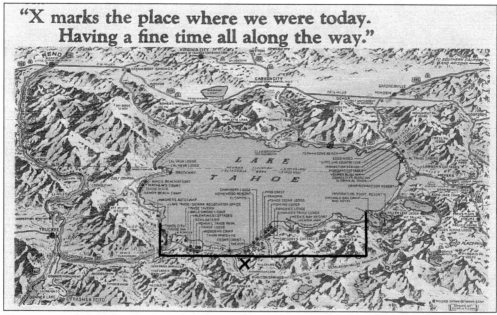

"X marks the place where we were today.
Having a fine time all along the way."

This vintage bird's-eye view of the Lake Tahoe area identifies the many hostelries and points of interest visitors could enjoy at Lake Tahoe, California and Nevada, c. 1920. This beautiful lake has been alternately known as *dewʔá:gaʔa* or *dáʔaw* in the Washoe language, "Lake Bonpland" by John C. Fremont, "Lake Tahoe" by Hubert H. Bancroft, and "Lake Bigler" by the State of California. The California legislature finally rescinded the 1870 legislation in 1945 and returned the lake to the name it is known by today. People have enjoyed its beauty from prehistoric to contemporary times. Please ensure to "Keep Tahoe Blue!" (Author's collection.)

CONTENTS

FOREWORD

Somewhere, over the rainbow, way up high,
There's a land that I heard of once in a lullaby.

—E.Y. Harburg, "Somewhere Over the Rainbow"

Some places have such inherent magic that it is difficult to believe they are in fact real. These places inspire the creation of places of fable: Oz (at least the Emerald City portion), Brigadoon, and Utopia. All these could have been created from a visit to Lake Tahoe's West Shore. This shore of California's fabled lake has witnessed and housed more movers and shakers—watching the surreal indigo and turquoise waters lapping at the shore on a bright summer afternoon—than one might at first suppose. These movers and shakers have been geologic as well as human. From ancient seismic activity to modern times, this region has been formed by high drama. Most recently, decades back rather than millennia, a substantial landslide formed today's avalanche zone at Emerald Bay. These same forces formed the West Shore's plentiful resources, which drew so many settlers starting in the late 19th century and continuing today. From lumber barons to cattle ranchers to gold miners, they have all found varying degrees of fortune on Tahoe's West Shore. Other human movers and shakers experienced professional turning points here. Mark Twain advised, "To breathe the air the angels breathe, go to Tahoe." John Steinbeck penned his first novel here, Wells Fargo president Isaias Hellman brokered a major water rights agreement with William Mulholland here, Frank Lloyd Wright was moved to propose daring designs here, Henry Kaiser built his Fleur de Lac estate here, and the list goes on and on. And all of these came after generations of Washoe people had resided here for millennia (and some still do). Even the wintertime is magic, as the organizers of the 1960 Olympic Games discovered when they set the first Olympic biathlon competition on the West Shore at Ed Z'berg Sugar Pine Point State Park. The images assembled in this book will transport you to another world and other times, taking you to a land of enchantment that, unlike so many, really exists. The popular bumper sticker proclaims, "West Shore is the best shore!" and on a languid summer day, or even a frigid winter day of frozen drama, its magical draw is unlike any other.

—Marguerite Sprague
Executive Director
North Lake Tahoe Historical Society

ACKNOWLEDGMENTS

Warm appreciation to the following for providing family reminiscences and images: Karri Samson, the Doctor Harvey and Lois Perman family, the Peter and Vita Normann family, and the Rasmus and Dorothy Jensen family.

A debt of thanks is owed also to the following organizations and their staff members: Wil Jorae, California Department of Parks and Recreation; Jesse Hadley and Christine Shook, Tahoe Maritime Museum; Susan Snyder and James Eason, Bancroft Library; David Tirman, JMA Ventures LLC; Marguerite Sprague, North Lake Tahoe Historical Society; Kathleen Correia, California State Library; Jeff Thomas, San Francisco History Center–San Francisco Public Library; Cara Randall, California State Railroad Museum; Debra Kaufman, California Historical Society; Mary Cory and John McCabe, El Dorado County Museum; and Katherine Barker, Tahoe Yacht Club. Thank you to Arcadia Publishing acquisitions editor John Poultney and publisher Tiffany Frary for their continuing interest in California history. The errors and omissions in the writing are all mine.

Members of the San Francisco Bay Area Postcard Club (www.postcard.org) have been most helpful and added images from their personal collections for inclusion. My gratitude is extended to club members Ken Prag, of San Francisco; Dorothy De Mare, of Petaluma; and Jack Hudson, of Dublin.

Finally, many individuals have been most generous in their encouragement and support. Michael and Liliane Silver graciously opened their home to me. The staff at PDQ Market, Tahoma, sustains me, and Susan Gearhart inspires me. Frances Dinkelspiel came to the rescue with personal Ehrman family photographs. Steve Zeleny and the Foursquare Church archive embraced the opportunity to tell the story of Sister Aimee at Tahoe-Cedars with true Christian generosity. The aid and patience of the irreplaceable Robert D. Haines Jr. cannot be overstated. Writing is impossible without the excellent and thorough copy editor extraordinaire Marcy Protteau.

All images are from my personal collection except where indicated. The following organizations and collections generously allowed the use of their images: Bancroft Library, University of California, Berkeley (BANC); Carpe Diem Fine Books, Monterey (CD); California Historical Society, San Francisco (CHS); California Department of Parks and Recreation, Photo Archive, Sacramento (CPR); California State Library, California History Room, Sacramento (CSL); Dorothy De Mare, private collection (DD); Frances Dinkelspiel, private collection (FD); El Dorado County Museum, Placerville (EDCM); Foursquare Church, Heritage Center Archive, Los Angeles (FSC); Jack Hudson, private collection (JH); Ken Prag, private collection (KP); US Library of Congress, Washington, DC (LOC); North Lake Tahoe Historical Society, Tahoe City (NLTHS); Rick Brower, private collection (RB); Harvey and Lois Perman, private collection (HP); California State Railroad Museum, Sacramento (RRM); the Betty and Karri Samson family, private collection (SF); San Francisco Public Library, History Room, San Francisco (SFPL); David A. Tirman, AIA, private collection (TIR); and the Tahoe Maritime Museum, (TMM).

The Lake Tahoe Sierra Association was the chamber of commerce organization of its day for the West Shore. The full-color brochure emphasizes the beauty of the lake and the many recreational opportunities along its shore. The organization's moving spirit was the Tahoe Tavern operation at Tahoe City. (KP.)

INTRODUCTION

Lake Tahoe's West Shore embraces its full ecological, economic, family, and spiritual histories. A casual visitor today experiences the same emotional response to the water, air, forest, and natural beauty that drew Native Americans, explorers, and entrepreneurs to the lake. Each arrives with his or her own desires and perceptions: the Washoe for alpine retreat, the Argonaut for mineral resources, the family to build a future, the worker for a respite, and the spiritual for God's grace.

The natural resources in the Tahoe Basin are vast. The Washoe people followed the retreating snows to summer on the West Shore where they collected pine nuts, fished for trout, and hunted small animals. Shallow estuaries provided commercial ice-making opportunities. Azorean commercial anglers pulled lake trout and mackinaw trout for shipping to both coasts, and small mining operations struggled near Quail Lake. In the 19th century, Tahoe was dominated by the timber industry. Surprisingly, today's tourism and hospitality industries are even larger than the timber industry was. It turns out that people are the greatest resource after all.

Duane L. Bliss and his business partners understood that natural resources encompass much more than gold and silver claims. Timber and forest-reserve claims are equally valuable. Gold mining in California's Mother Lode was primarily a placer operation requiring minimal skill, a pan, a shovel, and a little water to collect ore mostly from the earth's surface. The gold and silver strikes of Nevada's Comstock Lode were in hard rock and thus necessitated underground mining that required financial investment, sophisticated tunneling, engineering, and compressed-air machinery. Steam-engine power was required along every step of the process from lifting material 2,000 feet to extracting valuable ore from the overburden and junk rock. Key to this operation was timber for square-set support of the mineshafts; wood to burn in the steam locomotives, donkey engines, and power plants; and lumber for miners' homes, cooking, and comfort.

The D.L. Bliss business operations secured control of 50,000 acres of timber ringing Lake Tahoe's shores. The lumber mill at Glenbrook, Nevada, provided the basic ingredients for mining success on contract to the Ophir, Yellow Jacket, Gould, and Curry Consolidated Virginia and California mines and the Sutro Tunnel operations of Gold Hill, Virginia City, Silver City, and Dalton, Nevada. Their timber clear-cutting practices all but denuded the West Shore. Timber was often flumed into the lake, boomed together, and floated to the mill at Glenbrook. Timber stands located away from the shore were transported over narrow gauge short lines onto railroad piers. From there, the crop was boomed and transported to Glenbrook.

In a mining world powered by fire, the Bliss family success in the forest-product industry continued beyond the 1875 peak productivity of the Comstock mines. By 1890, both the available timber and the demand from the Comstock Lode were drawing to an economic end. All the mines in Story County, Nevada, were at minimal production. The population of the state had dropped so low that many in the east thought Nevada's statehood and disproportional Congressional representation should be withdrawn. D.L. Bliss looked for a new economic resource. He found it in land sales and development. Taking a cue from "Lucky" Baldwin and his successful Tallac House, the Bliss family saw the potential of human resources. With that knowledge, they set out to create and profit from the West Shore hospitality industry.

Staff and operations of Bliss's company were moved to 40 acres of non-logged property in Tahoe City where the Truckee River flowed from Lake Tahoe. The Lake Tahoe Railway & Transportation Company was incorporated in San Francisco on December 19, 1898, for the purposes of owning and operating a 16-mile railroad to Truckee, three miles of siding, steamers, and a hotel. The head office was 1280 Flood Building, San Francisco. The officers and directors were primarily C.T., D.L., D.L. Jr., W.D, and C.W. Bliss with capital shares authorized and outstanding of $500,000.

A land survey for laying a spur track to connect with the Central Pacific Railroad at the town of Truckee was commissioned. Track and sleepers from South Shore were ripped up and transported to the new center of operations: Tahoe City. Steamships were commissioned at the Union Iron Works in San Francisco, and rolling stock from Glenbrook was barged across the lake. Duane Bliss's son Walter Danforth Bliss was an architect and designed plans for the instant five-star resort Tahoe Tavern.

With its 40 miles of shoreline, the West Shore had residential and commercial potential. Parcels of land were purchased by prominent San Francisco families in part for speculation and in part to build family compounds. Religious organizations found land prices reasonable for purchase and improvement as summer campground retreats. Small family hotels, which were safe for single women and offered tent camping, reasonable rooms, and American Plan meals for families, dotted the shore. All of these hotels were accessible during the summer season with steamships that met train travelers at Tahoe City.

The first automobiles found their way to Tahoe in 1910. Navigating the unpaved roads on the overland trip required spare tires, an air pump, a patch kit, and tow chains. The road connecting Tahoe City to the Lake Tahoe Wagon Road (Highway 50) and known later as the Lincoln Highway or California Highway 89 was not completely graded and paved until the 1920s. Automobile access was limited to the summer season, but it brought an additional tourist segment to the lake with new demands for automobile camps and motels. Gasoline for the internal combustion engine supplanted wood as fuel for steam engines. Tree felling was stopped, and trains could now fill up with gasoline at the halfway point: Obexer's in Homewood.

Outreach to those not familiar with Lake Tahoe came with its discovery by the movie industry and the evangelical church from Los Angeles. Buster Keaton filmed silent movies along the Truckee River, one of his favorite "on-location" sites. The waters of the lake are the featured backdrop for young love, Royal Canadian Mounted Police adventures, and mafia murders. While the movies enticed visitors to the lake, religious groups also attempted to draw people to the West Shore. Aimee Semple McPherson envisioned the Tahoe-Cedars project in Tahoma as a summer camp retreat for the Foursquare Church in 1927. Charismatic and evangelical minister Sister Aimee actively promoted this development on the scale of the Methodist retreat camp at Pacific Grove, California. Once Los Angeles discovered San Francisco's retreat, the world wanted to visit too.

Tahoe's opportunities for tourism and recreation increased with the advent of winter sports. The Tahoe Tavern led the way with construction of snow play areas and encouragement of local ski teams. This new "second season" brought people to Truckee and Tahoe for snow play, tobogganing, skiing, ski jumping, and ice-skating. Recreational skiing gained in popularity after World War II, ensuring year-round tourism.

Year-round tourism with year-round support has its own environmental consequences. More families live and visit the Lake Tahoe Basin than ever before. Over 50,000 people live in the basin year-round. The tourist population can add in excess of 100,000 individuals per weekend day. Lodging, recreation, retail, food, and dining are the largest employment and revenue sources for the West Shore. While the tourism industry has increased year after year bringing money to the Tahoe Basin, the forest resources have returned to some degree after 100 years of recovery from Comstock logging. Lumbering ceased in the basin decades ago, and there have been few major fires; the forest is now a succession ecosystem comprising of Douglas fir and dense brush with a relatively low amount of sugar pines and incense cedar.

Organizations—like the Sierra Club, the League to Save Lake Tahoe, and Friends of the West Shore—are doing their part to ensure Lake Tahoe continues to be an ecologically and economically flourishing place through the 21st century and beyond. Private citizens, nonprofit organizations, and government agencies are working to ensure that Lake Tahoe and its surrounding lands retain their beauty and ecological status while the local economy is able to thrive.

One

Natural Resources

The history of Lake Tahoe's West Shore from its Native American habitation to earliest Euro-American discovery is centered on the abundant natural resources that the Tahoe Basin has to offer. The Washoe people of Carson Valley, Nevada, have summered in the Tahoe region for millennia to seek refuge from the summer valley heat. The Washoe spend their time in Tahoe hunting, fishing, weaving, and enjoying life.

The great pathfinder John C. Fremont and his corps of cartographers, scouts, and infantry first sighted the lake in February 1844 as part of their US Congress–funded exploration of the West. Fremont sighted the lake, but it was his cartographer's map indicating "gold found here" that began the Gold Rush. The rush was on to California after Pres. James K. Polk addressed Congress in December 1848. The Rush to Washoe followed in 1859.

The Gold Rush and subsequent Comstock Lode discovery set the stage for Lake Tahoe's natural resources to be developed. Money could be made in the mines, but wealth could also be derived from supplying the mines. Lake Tahoe held the forestry wealth necessary to supply the Virginia City, Gold Hill, and Dalton mining industry. Timber beams shored the mines with square-set supports, allowing mines to burrow thousands of feet into Mount Davidson. No coal seams exist in the Sierra Nevada range to use as fuel sources, but timber was bountiful. Trees were burned exclusively to create steam-powered mammoth pumps, winches, and stamp machines. From 1871, Duane L. Bliss and his associates controlled or owned 50,000 acres of forestlands encircling Lake Tahoe, which were felled in contract to the mines.

By 1890, the "Big Bonanza's" ore yield had come to the end of its economic viability; there were no longer any mining centers left in northern Nevada. From a population height of 25,000 people in Story County, Nevada, only 3,500 remained in 1900. Most of the mining leaders took their money and left. Bliss, headquartered in Glenbrook, Nevada, found himself without a market for timber and coincidentally out of timber reserves. He turned to land sales and development, as have so many timber companies. Duane L. Bliss and others sold the "spent" land for cash flow and developed a new "natural resource:" tourism.

Lake Tahoe, known to the Washoe people in their languages as *dewʔá:gaʔa* or *dáʔaw*, is located on the border of California and Nevada. It is a crystalline alpine lake more than 1,600 feet in depth, formed over two million years ago, and sculpted by volcanic and glacial action. It is ringed by the Sierra Nevada mountain range and provides vistas of spectacular natural beauty as seen in this 1928 photograph. (SFPL.)

The indigenous people of the Tahoe area are known as the Washoe people. They traditionally split their time between the Carson Valley and the Lake Tahoe West Shore. Small family groups spent the fall, winter, and spring seasons in the region between present-day Reno and Genoa, Nevada. Tahoe provided an escape from the valley heat in the summer, a change of scenery, and recreation opportunities much like those enjoyed by today's tourists. (LOC.)

Lt. John Charles Fremont (pictured) and his cartographer Charles Preuss are credited as the first Anglo-Europeans to view Tahoe from Red Lake Peak in the Carson Range, on February 14, 1844. Fremont was on a US government scouting expedition gathering geology, terrain, cartographic, and military information.

Washoe Native Americans are the indigenous Great Basin tribe that traditionally inhabits the Carson Valley and summers at Tahoe. They are linguistically and culturally unique from other tribes, notably the Paiute, in Nevada. Pinion pine nuts, acorns, grasses, small mammals, fish, and deer provided the basis of their hunter-gatherer lifestyle until the Europeans arrived and harvested the pine forests. (LOC.)

Clear-cutting of pinion pine forests, cattle grazing, fencing, and an influx of Anglo-Europeans into the Carson Valley ruined the forest habitat in the Tahoe Basin and forced many Washoe into ranch jobs and domestic roles. It became common to see Washoe families at Tahoe and onboard ships. A summer tourist snapped an image of this Washoe woman with her child cradled on her back. Seeing a Native American in the 20th century, long after the frontier was settled, was a romantic throwback. (KP.)

Many Washoe are expert basket weavers. Baskets are made for every domestic use from grain storage, to cooking, to quivers. Willow switches, stripped of leaves and divided, provide the basic weaving material. Bracken ferns, California quail top feathers, and natural dyes help to create the patterns. Collectors consider Washoe basketry the finest of all North American tribes. Dat So La Le (legal name Louisa Keyser, 1829?–1925), pictured here, is acclaimed for this art form. (NLTHS.)

14

For millennia, humans have occupied Tahoe City, located where the Truckee River leaves Lake Tahoe. Washoe tribes camped here in the summer, and Anglo-Europeans stopped here en route from mining operations in Squaw Valley to Carson City/Virginia City. This early sketch from *Vischer's Views of California* is the earliest known image of Tahoe City and dates from September 1865. (CHS.)

The Squaw Valley mines were exhausted by 1864, ending a short-lived boom of hard-rock mining. Investors in the area then shifted from mining claims to timber claims. The lifeblood of the mining industry was wood to burn, brace, and build. The mountains surrounding Lake Tahoe were dense with Douglas fir, incense cedar, and sugar, Jeffrey, and pinion pines. (SFPL.)

Forests were clear-cut and flumed down dry slides from great elevations. Momentum would allow the timber to travel long distances before dropping into a river or lake. Heat from the great friction generated by the logs as they traveled would often set the dry wooden slide and surrounding forest on fire. (NLTHS.)

A trail of smoke follows the log as it is delivered into the water. This is not fog or steam rising on a brisk winter morning. The log may actually have been on fire as it reached the water. After the logs made it to the water, they were boomed together and barged to Glenbrook or Incline Village. (CPR.)

The vast amount of timber clear-cut from the Tahoe area is hard to visualize until viewing this Truckee River scene: the bare mountainside, the milled lumber, and the railroad built to transport it. This image shows the completed narrow gauge railroad spur from Tahoe City to Truckee. The crew, equipment, rolling stock, and locomotive have all been transported from Glenbrook, Nevada, to Tahoe City, California. It takes a lot of lumber to build a hotel, staff accommodations, water storage, a power station, and out buildings. The nondescript, workhorse Baldwin locomotive was renamed No. 1 Tahoe and would soon carry passengers to a new recreation destination along the shores of Lake Tahoe. In the meantime, No. 1's job was to haul the freshly milled lumber to build a new hostelry at the end of the line: the Tahoe Tavern. (CPR.)

Samuel Clemens (pen name Mark Twain) had visions of riches as he and his associate John Kinney visited Lake Tahoe to stake a timber claim. Clemens's recollections are spun into a tale in *Roughing It* (1872). As he plans to exploit the natural riches, aspirations of becoming a timber magnate soon spin into dreamy days in a boat marveling at the crystal clarity of Tahoe's water.

A US Coast Guard–built lighthouse was maintained and illuminated nightly on Lake Tahoe from 1916. It was located on Rubicon Point, less than one mile from Pomin's Resort. Its location and maintenance is not surprising, as Capt. Joe Pomin was the captain of the steamship SS *Tahoe* and proprietor of Pomin's Resort. The light, but not this building, was moved north from Rubicon Point to Sugar Pine Point in 1921 and used as an aid to navigation until 1935. (CPR.)

Kentucky native William "General" Phipps
(birth sometime around 1813 and death
sometime around 1883–1887) was the first
to homestead 160 acres at Sugar Pine Point,
constructing his home in approximately
1860. It was lost to fire, and a second home
was built in approximately 1872. Phipps
later sold the property to M.H. de Young.
William Lapham later constructed the
short-lived Hotel Bellevue on the site. The
second Phipps cabin still stands today at Ed
Z'berg Sugar Pine Point State Park. (CPR.)

Duane Leroy Bliss (1833–1907) essentially
created the Lake Tahoe West Shore as it
is known today. His firms—Yerington,
Bliss & Co., and the Carson and Tahoe
Lumber and Fluming Company—began
buying Tahoe timberland in the early
1870s. In the 1890s, Bliss changed his
industry focus from logging, milling,
and transportation to hospitality,
tourism, and transportation. (CSL.)

Noted San Francisco landscape photographer Carleton Watkins (1829–1916) visited Lake Tahoe in the late 1870s and took a series of pictures. He is often credited with popularizing the Sierra Nevada and Yosemite. This image is identified as, "Near Tahoe City Cal (Embarcadero) [Steamer at dock, by the Custom House, Lake Tahoe] ca. 1878?" Watkins later used details of this image in his stereograph No. 4010. (BANC.)

Tahoe City did not change much during its first 30 years. This image was taken around 1898, prior to the Tahoe Tavern construction. Railroad tracks circle the customs house and piers. Forest appears at lake level, but stripped mountainsides are visible in the distance. (NLTHS.)

Erected by A.J. Bayley in 1871, the Grand Central Hotel was the first luxury hotel built in Tahoe City. It exceeded in popularity the Glenbrook House (established in 1863), which had catered to Virginia City magnates. The Grand Central functioned as the stage stop through a succession of proprietors. The hotel provided Wells Fargo banking and stage services as well. (CSL.)

Originally known as the Tahoe House, the Tahoe Hotel was built by William Pomin in 1864. Robert Montgomery Watson purchased it in 1880 and renamed it the Tahoe Hotel. This rare business card welcomes visitors, extolling the resort's attractions. Tahoe Inn seen today is the result of a succession of fires and rebuilding. (KP.)

This early photographic image mounted on cardboard shows the Grand Central Hotel in its summer and winter aspects c. 1886. The hotel boasted rugs, mahogany furniture, and an iron stove. It had accommodations worthy of the first adventurous women to enjoy the Lake Tahoe scenery during the winter of 1869. (BANC.)

This rare Tahoe House Stage Line ticket would have secured travelers a seat via the Truckee River route to connect with the Central Pacific Railroad in Truckee. The 16-mile journey by six-horse team would have taken up to three hours depending on the condition of the road. (TMM.)

Two

DESTINATION RESORT

While most of those who made their millions left the Comstock Lode to reinvest or enjoy their wealth elsewhere, the Bliss family stayed in Tahoe. Their operations were moved from Glenbrook, Nevada, on the southeastern edge of the lake to Tahoe City, California, located on the northwestern shore. Rolling stock, train crews, lumbermen, craftsmen, and equipment were floated across the lake to create a new enterprise. A workhorse, narrow gauge locomotive was saved from scrap, renumbered, and renamed engine No. 1 Tahoe. The locomotive would run on the new short line along the Truckee River and connect with the Central Pacific Railroad transcontinental route at the Truckee depot. From there, it was a memorable scenic trip to the Tahoe City railroad pier where the SS *Tahoe* waited. This steamship, which held 200 people, was built at the Union Iron Works in San Francisco and launched at Glenbrook in 1894.

As the largest hamlet on the Northwest Shore, Tahoe City accommodated people traveling along the lakeshore between Truckee and "Virginny" (Nevada) with a stage stop and the year-round Tahoe House hotel. Bliss had a more ambitious plan when he moved his operations to Tahoe City. Survey and engineering for what was envisioned as a destination resort commenced in 1898. The Tahoe Tavern hotel opened for business for the summer season in 1902. This beautiful hostelry designed by architect Walter Danforth Bliss, son of Duane L. Bliss, boasted rooms for 450 guests, steam heat, telephone and telegraph service, electricity, private baths, and every modern amenity. The $500,000 loan secured to create the 40-acre resort property was worth the investment. Tahoe Tavern was an instant five-star success.

Recreational options at Tahoe Tavern included horseback riding, 10-pin bowling, a swimming pool, ballroom dancing, fishing, and an open-air Episcopal chapel. An additional 60-room annex was completed in 1906. A second floor was added in 1907 to incorporate a casino, barbershop, and ballroom with stage. Construction continued over the next 20 years and included the addition of a bar with the end of Prohibition, new garages with the advent of the automobile, and the addition of more and more guest rooms. In the 1920s, the resort began opening for the winter season and offered skiing, sleigh rides, tobogganing, and other snow sports. The good times at Tahoe Tavern continued for over 60 years until its closure in 1964.

Engine No. 3 Glenbrook, of the Carson and Tahoe Lumber and Fluming Company, was built in 1877 by the Baldwin Locomotive works. The engine found new life in 1898 as one of four locomotives for the Lake Tahoe Railway & Transportation Company. This narrow gauge locomotive at first hauled lumber to build the Tahoe Tavern, the railroad pier, and auxiliary buildings. After the Tavern opened, the Glenbrook brought guests from the Central Pacific Truckee depot to Tahoe City. (NLTHS.)

1917   **LAKE TAHOE**   N°. 384

RAILWAY & TRANSPORTATION COMPANY

PASS Mr. & Mrs. M. F. Van Horn,
Dist. Passenger Agent,
Pennsylvania Lines.
OVER ENTIRE SYSTEM

UNTIL DECEMBER 31ST 1917   UNLESS OTHERWISE ORDERED AND SUBJECT TO CONDITIONS ON BACK

VALID WHEN COUNTERSIGNED BY MYSELF OR C. W. NELSON
COUNTERSIGNED BY

VICE PRESIDENT & GEN. MGR.

This rare annual pass for unlimited transport over the Lake Tahoe Railway & Transportation Company, organized on December 19, 1898, is a unique remaining piece of railroad ephemera. The system in this instance consisted only of travel both ways between Truckee and Tahoe City. It was common for railroads to extend reciprocity to other railroad company agents. The Pennsylvania line at this time was the largest railroad in the nation. (KP.)

The narrow gauge track extended beyond the Tahoe Tavern railroad wharf with spurs terminating at Squaw Valley, Customs House, and Ward Creek. This early image shows the cave where the Washoe people collected swallow eggs—one of the natural food attractions of the area. This is one of the first locations where Anglo-Europeans encountered the Washoe in the Tahoe Basin. The cave and the train tracks are now underwater. (NLTHS.)

LAKE TAHOE RAILWAY & TRANSPORTATION COMPANY

CONDITIONS

This pass may be revoked at any time, and if presented by any other person than the individual named hereon, or if any alteration, addition or erasure is made upon it, it is forfeited and the conductor or purser will take it up and collect full fare. This is a free pass based upon no consideration whatsoever. The person accepting and using this pass, in consideration of receiving the same, agrees that the

LAKE TAHOE RAILWAY & TRANSPORTATION COMPANY

shall not be liable under any circumstances, whether of negligence— criminal or otherwise—of its agents or others, for any injury to the person, or for any loss or damage to the property of the individual using this pass; and that as to such person the Company shall not be considered as a common carrier or liable as such.

I hereby assent to the above statements, and hereby agree that this pass is subject to the above conditions, that I will make my signature whenever required by the Company's agents or conductors and will not use this pass in violation of any State or Federal law.

I also state that I am not prohibited by law from receiving free transportation and that this pass will be lawfully used.

M. H. Van Horn

(Sign in ink)

The reverse of this annual pass shows the signature of M.H. Van Horn, the Pennsylvania Line passenger agent for Los Angeles, who was appointed in 1906. Carrying more traffic and generating more revenue in the early 20th century than any other railroad, the Pennsylvania Railroad had investments in many railroads throughout the United States. (KP.)

The Tahoe Tavern opened in 1902 after two years of planning and construction at a reputed cost of $150,000. The Bliss family had experience in the hospitality industry as the proprietors of the Glenbrook House, located on the southeastern shore near their lumber mill operations. The Glenbrook House, later renamed Glenbrook Inn and Ranch, catered to the wealthy, just as was intended for the Tahoe Tavern. (SFPL.)

Because of its remote location, the Tahoe Tavern was completely self-contained. Wood-fueled, steam-powered generators created electricity for illumination, hot water, onsite laundry, and public room heating. Drinking water required construction of two reservoirs on the distant Burton Creek with a gravity-driven water pipe for delivery. (KP.)

The tourism year at Tahoe Tavern began as the snow melted and locomotives could travel the rail line. The resort was a seasonal affair at first and could accommodate 1,000 visitors at any time in its four-story hotel and cabins. The 40-acre facility employed a full staff, including a recreational specialist for every interest and chefs to provide delicious meals. All of the modern conveniences were consistently brought up to date with the latest fashion. (DD.)

The tavern created and held a captive clientele for approximately 15 years until the advent of the automobile. The leisure to just sit on a veranda and enjoy the surroundings was part of the recreational appeal of the property. Pencils, fountain pens, telegraph, and telephone were the only means of communication. (DD.)

DINING ROOM,
TAHOE TAVERN,
LAKE TAHOE

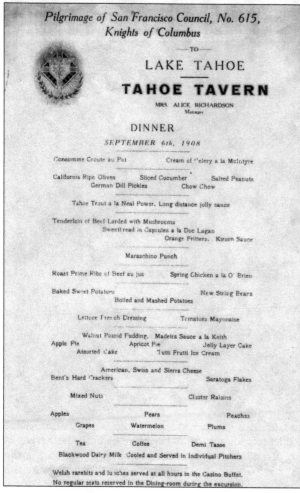

Pilgrimage of San Francisco Council, No. 615,
Knights of Columbus

— TO —

LAKE TAHOE

TAHOE TAVERN

MRS. ALICE RICHARDSON
Manager

DINNER

SEPTEMBER 6th, 1908

Consomme Croute au Pot   Cream of Celery a la McIntyre

California Ripe Olives   Sliced Cucumber   Salted Peanuts
German Dill Pickles   Chow Chow

Tahoe Trout a la Neal Power, Long distance jolly sauce

Tenderloin of Beef Larded with Mushrooms
Sweetbread in Capsules a la Doc Lagan
Orange Fritters, Kirsch Sauce

Maraschino Punch

Roast Prime Ribs of Beef au jus   Spring Chicken a la O' Brien

Baked Sweet Potatoes   New String Beans
Boiled and Mashed Potatoes

Lettuce French Dressing   Tomatoes Mayonaise

Walnut Pound Pudding, Madeira Sauce a la Keith
Apple Pie   Apricot Pie   Jelly Layer Cake
Assorted Cake   Tutti Frutti Ice Cream

American, Swiss and Sierra Cheese
Bent's Hard Crackers   Saratoga Flakes

Mixed Nuts   Cluster Raisins

Apples   Pears   Peaches
Grapes   Watermelon   Plums

Tea   Coffee   Demi Tasse
Blackwood Dairy Milk Cooled and Served in Individual Pitchers

Welsh rarebits and lunches served at all hours in the Casino Buffet.
No regular seats reserved in the Dining-room during the excursion.

Meals were served on the American Plan, which was three meals served every day and included in the price of the room. This plan was common at all the resorts at Lake Tahoe and is still common in Europe and remote regions where other dining options are not available. (KP.)

Special railroad excursions and fraternal organization meetings drew visitors to the tavern as the summer tourist season concluded. The male-only Knights of Columbus organization enjoyed a fraternal weekend in September 1908. No prices are listed on this menu, as meals were included in the daily room rate. (NLTHS.)

The brisk Lake Tahoe water temperature may have been too cold or intimidating for some, but there was always the pool. In 1930, visitors could watch the train arrive to rendezvous with the steamship, order lunch, enjoy a beverage, watch people, and most enjoyably of all, take in a view of the lake. (KP.)

The game of 10-pin bowling was a new feature at the tavern in 1907 when the six alleys were installed. Pin boys would clear and reset the pins; mechanical pin-setting did not come about until 1952. The mineralite balls shown here were introduced in 1914, dating this image probably to the 1920s. (KP.)

Modern visitors approaching Tahoe City from the south would hardly recognize the number of trees, the rural aspect, and the unpaved road leading to the entrance of the Tahoe Tavern. Signs indicating access to modern conveniences, such as the telephone and Western Union, were important. After all, Tahoe Tavern had the only telephone along the North and West Shores in 1902. (DD.)

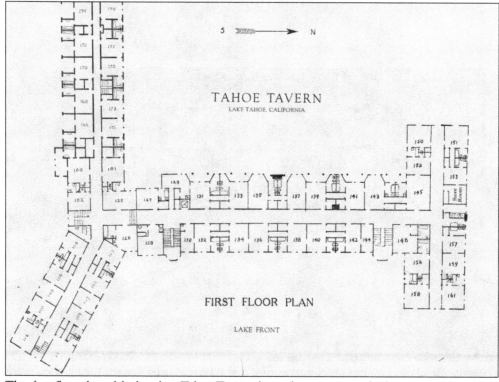

This first-floor plan of the hotels at Tahoe Tavern shows that every room had open-air access. Even today, having a lake or garden view is common in resort room reservations and pricing. Integration of the hotel into the natural experience was a conscious architectural design element. (NLTHS.)

TAHOE TAVERN

LAKE TAHOE, CALIFORNIA

Opening Saturday, June 11th, 1932

SPORTS PROGRAM

Fishing, Swimming, Boating.
Horseback Riding, Dancing.
Motion Pictures, Bowling and Billiards.

GOLF COURSE

All Grass Greens and Fairways Automatically Sprinkled

RATES PER DAY

American Plan Only

Rooms without bath, 1 person	$ 7.00 to $ 9.00
Rooms without bath, 2 persons	11.00 to 13.00
Rooms with bath, 1 person	9.00 to 12.00
Rooms with bath, 2 persons	14.00 to 18.00

Special Rates to Families

Pullman Accommodations via Southern Pacific Direct to Tahoe Tavern

For Reservations and Information, Address:

E. C. ROGERS, Resident Manager,
Tahoe Tavern, Lake Tahoe, Calif.

MATT GREEN, Lessee and General Manager

Descriptive matter and reservations without charge at Peck-Judah Travel Bureaus
Please mention Peck-Judah when writing this Resort

Page 83

The Great Depression and the ascendancy of automobile transportation and culture both affected tavern occupancy. The hotel was no longer an exclusive destination resort with train transportation its only feeder. In 1924, the narrow gauge railroad connecting the Tahoe Tavern to Truckee was sold to the Southern Pacific Railroad, which assigned its mighty promotions department to entice ridership and year-round tourism. Other Bliss family investments suffered as a result of the 1929 stock market crash, precipitating more land sales throughout the 1930s. George Whittell Jr. (1881–1969) purchased 27 miles of Nevada shoreline (approximately 14,600 acres) from the Bliss family in 1938. Other properties long depleted of marketable timber were sold, and the Bliss family averted cash flow problems for the moment. (KP.)

The Tahoe Tavern was designed by San Francisco architect Walter Danforth Bliss (1872–1956). Bliss was the son of Duane Leroy Bliss, the timber, mining, and hospitality magnate, and designed the building for his family. A graduate of Massachusetts Institute of Technology in 1895, architect Bliss first worked for the architectural firm of McKim, Mead, and White in New York. Bliss and his friend and collaborator William Baker Faville (1866–1946), worked together to form their

Tahoe Tavern and LAKE TAHOE.

own architectural firm in San Francisco in 1889. Together, they secured major San Francisco architectural projects, such as the St. Francis Hotel (1904) and the Bank of California (1908). Together, they introduced the Shingle Style of architecture popular on the East Coast and in the Bay Area. This style sought to protect natural beauty by harmonizing with the landscape—a favorite theme of the Arts and Crafts movement. (KP.)

The Chapel of the Pines, also known as the Chapel of the Transfiguration, became the summer location for St. Nicolas Episcopal Church in Tahoe City. An original part of the Tahoe Tavern grounds, the chapel was the first church built in Tahoe City. It is listed in the National Register of Historic Places and has been in continuous use as a chapel since its construction in 1909. (KP.)

In addition to its hotel rooms, the Tahoe Tavern offered open-air or tent accommodations for visitors. Harold A. Parker (1878–1930), proprietor of the Tahoe Tavern Photography Studio, was the resident summer photographer and provided real-photo postcards, landscape photography, ethnographic images, and advertising images, such as this one of a family enjoying a tenting vacation. His clean compositional style makes his original photographic work of Tahoe, the California Missions, and Yosemite very collectable.

Three

SAN FRANCISCO'S RETREAT

The opening of Lake Tahoe to seasonal visitors after the era of the Comstock Lode coincided with the prosperity of San Francisco's Victorian Age. Alternatively christened the "Gas Light Era" or the "Gilded Age," the Victorian Age was a time when San Franciscans enjoyed life in the largest and wealthiest city in the western United States. Mineral wealth from the Comstock Lode and Virginia City flowed down to San Francisco, and economic times were flush. Hotel housekeepers and capitalists alike engaged in stock speculation. Wages were high.

In Tahoe, D.L. Bliss continued in his managed steps in land sales and development. Prominent San Francisco families purchased land for retreats and long-term speculation (reasoning that trees would grow back). *San Francisco Chronicle* publisher M.H. De Young and Jewish immigrant and banker Isaias Hellman purchased parcels at Sugar Pine Point. Hellman built his elegant Pine Lodge for the construction cost of $5,000 in 1902. This striking home is still enjoyed today. Gravel and cement magnate Henry J. Kaiser purchased land at Tahoe Pines to create his lakefront estate Fleur du Lac. Herbert Fleishhacker, philanthropist and president of the Anglo California National Bank, built his home near Blackwood Canyon, aptly naming it Idyllwild. Quarter- or eighth-section parcels, often denuded of trees, were available at reasonable prices. Land once valued by board feet of lumber to the acre was now valued by linear feet of lake shoreline. The unharvested timber near the shore often could be cleared to produce a homesite, provide sufficient timber to build, and leave enough sugar pine for shade and scenery.

Schoolmarms, working people, and shopkeepers came to the West Shore for a chance to get away. Single women and men came looking for each other. Families arrived with their children, often setting a generational migration pattern to stay at their favorite hostelry. Visitors could stay at a small lakeside resort for a week on the American Plan (three meals per day), including train transportation and transfers from San Francisco, for as little as $45 in 1910. Once visitors made it to the lake, the water, air, and good times were all free. The seasonal summer economy boomed.

Dear Sister & all. I received your letter this morning. We are well and hope this find [sic] you all the same. As Ever Your sister Lucy. 6/26 1906.

This the boat we came on

Arriving at the lakeshore to step aboard the next leg of the journey was an anticipated part of the fun. Here, a traveler wrote, "Dear Sister & all. I received your letter this morning. We are well and hope this find [sic] you all the same. As ever your sister Lucy. 6/26/1906. Thes [sic] the boat we came on McKinneys Lake Tahoe Cal." (KP.)

The narrow gauge train, passenger cars, and steamer SS *Tahoe* shown in this image indicate the size of these conveyances on a human scale. The railroad wharf is the largest component of the image. The locomotive is only 26 tons unburdened and carries passengers and freight along a narrow gauge (three feet) road. It is dwarfed by the 152-ton, 168-foot, 200-person passenger ship. Both are Victorian-era amusements equivalent to today's Disneyland rides. (NLTHS.)

The railroad pier doubles as a pleasure promenade; visitors and the railroad share access. Electrical poles and wires extend to the boathouse at wharf end. The SS *Tahoe* met the Lake Tahoe Railway & Transportation Company train from Truckee on a regular, published schedule. (NLTHS.)

The SS *Tahoe* embarked daily at 9:10 a.m. to deliver mail and passengers to all resorts of call around the lake, including the Moana Villa. Ralphy Lewis Colwell built the Moana Villa in a dense grove of yellow pine in 1894. The property boasted a two-and-a-half-story lodge, cottages, tents, a bathing house, a clubhouse over the water, and a 500-feet pier used as a steamer landing. (KP.)

TAHOE TATTLER.

VOL. I.   TAHOE, SATURDAY, AUGUST 6 1881.   NO. 25

GRAND CENTRAL

Hotel.

THE CHOICEST SUMMER RESORT

IN THE STATE.

TAHOE, PLACER COUNTY, CAL.

A. J Bayley, : ; Prop.

HUNTER'S HOME.

SUGAR-PINE POINT, LAKE TAHOE, CAL.

Cottages for everybody. Free boats for guests. Good hunting and fishing.

J. W. McKinney : : Proprietor

TAHOE MARKET.

The best beef, pork and mutton to be had in the mountains constantly on hand.

J. P. Bayley : : Proprietor

MAYO & HURLEY.

SMALL BOATS FOR FISHING PARTIES

Always on Hand.

Orders left with either of the above named or at the office of the Grand Central Hotel will be promptly attended to.   jy-9tf

"MINNIE MOODY."

UNDER THE MANAGEMENT OF

Capt. Jas. Powell.

Parties desiring can charter this boat for fishing and pleasure excursions by the day or week. Fishing tackles on board.   jl-9tf

BILLIARDS.

ADJOINING THE GRAND CENTRAL.

Billiard room and bar with finest liquor of wines, liquors and cigars.

GOV. STANFORD.

THIS SIDE-WHEEL STEAMER, LLOYD Hawthorn, Business manager,

Leaves Tahoe every morning for a trip around the lake, stopping at all important places. Fare for round trip $4 and $2 across.

Joe Pomin,   Captain.

The key to the credibility of any city is the establishment of a local newsletter. The *Tahoe Tattler* was a handset, letterpress weekly advertising Tahoe City businesses and services. What sold the newspaper, then as now, were stories about the arrivals of celebrities, politicians, and other people of interest. This edition, dated August 6, 1881, notes the arrival, of judges, members of Congress, and mining magnates from Virginia City at the Grand Hotel, the toniest place in town. Notable is the mention of Mrs. George Hearst (Phoebe née Apperson), known for her largess and endowments to the University of California. George Hearst secured his first fortune in the Comstock Lode. He multiplied his fortune with the largest gold strike and mining operation in the world, the Homestake Mine in Black Hills, Montana. (Both, KP.)

Tahoe Tattler.

SATURDAY   Aug 6

JOTTINGS.

—We had the pleasure of making the acquaintance of B. H. Evans of the EXPRESS, Marysville; he will stop with us a while to recruit health.

—Many of the first month's subscriptions expire with the number. Parties interested will please take notice and renew.

—Carrie Stevenson and M T Benham, took in fifteen trout last evening as the result of one and a half hours fishing at Sunny Side.

—Miss. Anna Head, now stopping at the hotel, is one of the most noted lady swimmers of this coast, and if this fine weather lasts, she may try her skill in the lake, and thus refute the common idea that good swimmers are not able to navigate these waters. We shall be pleased to chronicle some of her exploits

—Do not forget the boat race at John Mc. Kinney's tomorow. There is to be lots of fun, anc some one is going to lose a hundred dollars.

—We wish to inform our inquiring exchange, that "venison" is the meat of animals of the CERVUS family.

G. C. Arrivals.

Hon. D O Mc. Kenney, Austin, Nev Hon. Richard Rising, wf. and dr. Miss Woods; Hon: W E F Deal, Virginia City; Col. D L Bliss, wf, and two drs. S W Waugh, Carson; W S Rayle, Gold Hill; Mrs. Geo. Hearst and servt. A E Head wf. and dr., Miss. Maggie Hamilton, Mrs. J Wrightman, H T Quinn, Geo. H Payne and wf., S. F.   A H Manning, Reno.

—J. P. Bayley saw two deer just over the bridge, a little ways back from the river, not more than a fourth of a mile from town. O ye hunters why do you not give us death notices in this line.

—H. C. Ewing of the Alabaster Cave, and the proprietary young ladies of the hotel, are making the tour of the lake to day. Hope the young gentleman can succeed in finding as much beauty in our region as his own.

—Sam'l. Woodman caught nine trout this morning before breakfast, at Mr. Kinney's.

—Byrne, of the Nevada Mint is now coining happiness at Hunters Home.

—A very large rattle snake was killed on the trail to Soda springs the other day four and a half feet long.

—Mrs. Mc. Murtrie and party have returned from Rubicon Soda springs.

Other than horse and wagon, the only mode of transport around the lake was steamship. The great wealth that built Victorian San Francisco came from the Nevada mines. Owning a home in San Francisco and a summer retreat or family compound at Lake Tahoe became very popular in the late 1890s and more so in 1900 with the advent of regular steam transportation. (NLTHS.)

Lake Tahoe became a seasonal vacation retreat for working people as well. Their newfound affluence in the economy of San Francisco and a release from year-round toil drew people from all strata of society. These five single women are en route to a week at Homewood Resort. (KP.)

Idyllwild is one of the private lakeshore residences passengers would have seen from the decks of the SS *Tahoe*; another is the Mortimer Fleishhacker estate, built by contractor Frederick Kehl in 1957. Idyllwild is near Blackwood Canyon and Eagle Rock at today's Tahoe Pines. (KP.)

Isaias W. Hellman (1842–1920) began purchasing acreage at Sugar Pine Point in 1897–1898 with an initial 1,000-acre parcel. He constructed Pine Lodge near the point in 1903 at a cost of $5,000. Pine Lodge architect Walter Danforth Bliss designed the Tahoe Tavern as well. The Hellman, Ehrman, and Lazard families enjoyed the compound until 1965 when it was acquired by the State of California.

Sidney M. Ehrman (1873–1974), son-in-law of Isaias Hellman, is shown on the pier at Sugar Pine Point posing with two of Lake Tahoe's famous Lahontan cutthroat trout. Ehrman (Hastings College of Law class of 1905) became senior partner of the San Francisco law firm Heller Ehrman White & McAuliffe. Ehrman was ever the well-dressed angler, denoted by the sports jacket, tie, khaki pants, and saddle loafer shoes. His wife, Florence Hellman Ehrman, would inherit Pine Lodge in 1920. (JD.)

On the front veranda of Pine Lodge, Mrs. Isaias Hellman (née Esther Newgass) and daughter Clara Hellman Heller (right) enjoy the day. Isaias and Esther married in New York on April 14, 1870. They had three children: Isaias William Jr., Clara, and Florence. Their great-grandson F. Warren Hellman (1934–2011), a private equity investor and San Francisco philanthropist, is the founder of Golden Gate Park Hardly Strictly Bluegrass music festival. (JD.)

The SS *Tahoe* during the summer and the *Meteor* during the winter served all points of call as well as regular and seasonal US post offices once a day throughout the year. This was a much-anticipated arrival, as all visitors and locals relied on the ships for freight, food supplies, and paying guests. (KP.)

Tahoma Resort was bereft of marketable timber when Joseph Bishop purchased the land from his brother-in-law and lumberman Augustus Colwell. The timber claim was stripped of logs and had zero economic value when Bishop acquired it. Cottages were constructed and run as a resort from 1916 to 1920. *Tahoma* is an invented word meaning "home away from home." (KP.)

The hotel at Homewood was a popular American Plan resort catering to families and groups of single women. Shown is a group of women friends on a weeklong vacation in 1911, shortly after the hotel was opened by Annien and Arthur Jost. (KP.)

Dancing was a popular diversion, and almost every hotel resort had an outside or covered dance floor. These dance pavilions continued their popularity into the 1960s with the advent of jukeboxes. This dance floor was adjacent to the Homewood Hotel and featured electrical illumination of Japanese paper lanterns. (KP.)

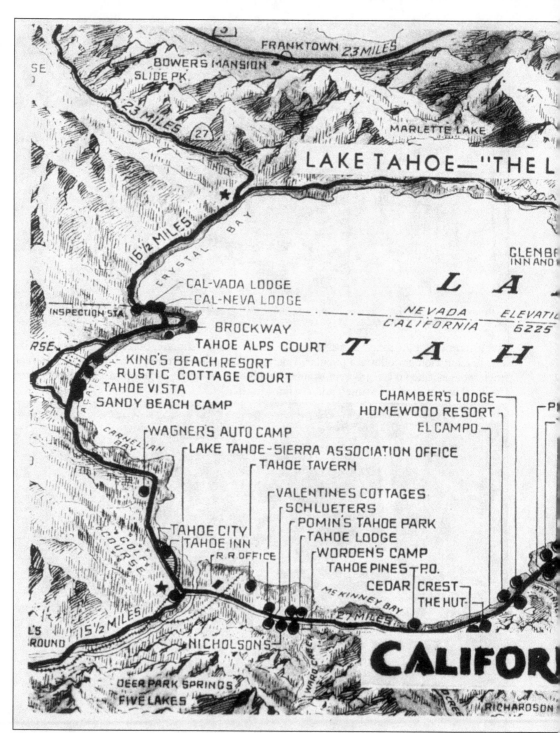

The Sierra Tahoe Association was the equivalent of a chamber of commerce for the Lake Tahoe West Shore. The association printed promotional brochures, engaged cartographers to create commercial maps of the region, and collaborated with the Southern Pacific Railroad to market special excursion events and pricing at local resorts. This 1930s map of Lake Tahoe graphically

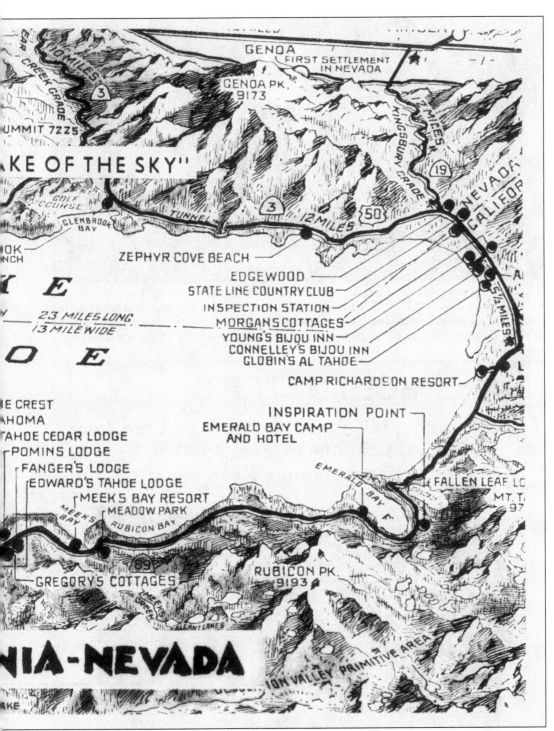

demonstrates the popularity of the West Shore. The 27 miles from the South Shore Y to Tahoe City, California, is peppered with over two dozen hostelries. The East Shore, Nevada, has only the Glenbrook Inn reserved by the Bliss family. The remaining 27 miles of the eastern lakeshore is owned entirely by George Whittell, of Thunderbird Lodge fame, for his personal enjoyment.

El Campo was a popular tent camping spot in the 1920s located between Homewood Resort and Chamber's Lodge. "Old Bill" Johnson, a former Sacramento blacksmith (known for his Prohibition-era moonshine dubbed "Sierra white lightning") owned and ran the summer camping property. Subsequently, the El Campo Inn, a favorite tourist lodge in the 1930s, was constructed on this site.

SCHLUETER'S

Located in the Tall Pines, in an Area Free from Poison Oak, Rattlesnakes, Wind and Uncomfortable Heat.

This brochure for Schlueter's Lodge, located south of Tahoe City, reads like a George Babbitt 1920s booster promotion for the area. Schlueter cuts to the chase: no rattlesnakes, no poison oak, and no heat. Lake Tahoe's West Shore is the perfect vacation destination. (KP.)

The Hut at Willowwood Camp advertises modern cabins in 1939 and promises good food, good drinks, and good times, according to the *Tahoe Tattler* newsletter of June 30, 1939. The proprietor, Ben Callender, proclaims a good "chance" for a good time (especially because he had a liquor license) as the Hut was built from lumber recycled from the Homewood (gambling) Casino. Gambling became legal in Nevada in 1931, essentially putting illegal West Shore casinos out of business. The Hut burned in 1955. (KP.)

Rowing was a pleasurable pastime for ladies as well as gentlemen before internal combustion engines or outboard motors were introduced. Appropriate rowing apparel included the long walking skirt, summer white blouse, and, of course, a fashionable hat. This real-photo postcard indicating "welcome back" from Walter suggests this was a regular, return vacation. (KP.)

Annien and Arthur Jost started the hotel at Homewood in 1910. This 1911 image shows the hotel at its rustic best. It continued as a hostelry for decades until Helen Alrich purchased it along with the adjacent Ski Hill. The building was torn down in 1963. (KP.)

R. Colwell acquired the Sugar Pine Point property from William "General" Phipps in 1889. On the property rose the Hotel Bellevue and cottages, functioning as a popular resort for only five years. Rates were $12–$15 per week or $2.50–$3 a day on the American Plan. Visitors could reach the Bellevue by stage via Rubicon Springs. Isaias Hellman subsequently purchased the land in 1887. (CPR.)

There was a resort accommodation along with West Shore for every budget. Homewood and Tahoma were very reasonable for families with children and working teachers or clerks from San Francisco. A Tahoe vacation was surprisingly affordable for all in the 1910s and 1920s. (KP.)

Sunnyside Resort and Boat Company was established just south of Tahoe City along Hurricane Bay in the early 1880s at the site of Saxton's old mill and wharf. The resort included cottages, a boathouse, and, of course, a pier. Modern-day visitors know this resort as Sunnyside Lodge and Steakhouse along the renamed Sunnyside Bay. (KP.)

Tourists would find a weeklong vacation at Chamber's Landing, including room, board, and roundtrip transportation from San Francisco all for $46. McKinney's Hunters Retreat, now renamed Chamber's Landing, was host to many early outdoorsmen. Most notable was John Muir, who described the sugar pines surrounding the resort as "priest of the forest extending their arms in benediction over the congregation." (KP.)

John Washington McKinney started what is known today as Chamber's Landing as McKinney's Hunters Retreat in 1863. He proclaimed it the finest hunting and fishing camp in the Sierra Nevada. McKinney, the colorful former mountain man, lost the retreat in 1892 over a $600 whiskey debt to William Westhoff, a "spirits drummer" from Sacramento. David Henry Chambers purchased McKinney's resort from the Westhoffs and renamed it Chamber's Lodge in 1920. (KP.)

LAKESHORE COTTAGES, CHAMBERS LODGE, LAKE TAHOE, CALIF.

The first boathouse on Tahoe was built at McKinney's in 1875. Boats were available to rent with or without outboard motors at reasonable rates at Chamber's Landing, originally known as McKinney's Hunters Retreat. Pleasure boat rides in powerful mahogany "woody" runabouts were the highlight of the vacation for many visitors. (KP.)

Chamber's Lodge continued to be a popular resort through the 1950s and still operates today (as Chamber's Landing). This Neher painting shows the car and boat accessibility of the resort in the 1930s. The dockside bar is noted for its signature adult beverage known as the "Chamber's punch." Pour into a silver bowl light rum and dark rum. Add orange and pineapple juice, sweet and sour, and grenadine for color. Finish with a floater of 151-proof rum. (KP.)

Frank and Marion Pomin (née Slade) established Pomin's Lodge in 1864. William Pomin had established the Tahoe House in Tahoe City in 1863. A US post office at Pomin's Lodge was established in 1915 and continued until 1945. It was moved and renamed the Tahoma Post Office after 1945. (KP.)

Pomin's accommodations were more rustic than those at Chamber's but reflected the popular Arts and Crafts style in its interior design. Integration of Japanese lanterns, Native American crafts, and nature into the interior space is combined with modern electric illumination. Pomin has a second resort located at today's Sunnyside Bay and beautifully restored as the Cottage Inn. (KP.)

Summer vacations along the West Shore soon became ritual family occasions, and many families returned to the same resort for generations. Here, three children—Alan, George, and Shirley—on the steps of their West Shore summer cabin c. 1950 are told, "Stand up straight, and I will take your picture."

Opening day is celebrated at Rubicon Park, now D.L. Bliss State Park, by Capt. Joe Pomin and the crew of the SS *Tahoe*. Rubicon Park and its hostelry Rubicon Lodge were a regular postal stop for the steamer operating from 1921 to 1931. George Newhall acquired the property for a family compound. He subsequently subdivided and developed the property. (CSL.)

The Meeks Bay Resort was one of the most popular resorts along the West Shore. George T. and James A. Murphy purchased the property for $250 in gold eagle coins in 1884. The brothers intended to purchase the land in 1878 but were preempted by D.L. Bliss, representing Carson and Tahoe Lumber and Fluming Company. Bliss promised the brothers they could purchase the land for their original offering price once the property had been logged. (KP.)

Very popular were the full horse-trail services offered by Meeks Bay Stables. Meeks Bay was originally a summer grazing pasture for cattle and milk cows. Equestrian-themed recreation was a natural extension. The stables opened around June 25 of each year. Meeks Bay is one of the few easily reached trails for horse access into the Desolation Wilderness back area. (SF.)

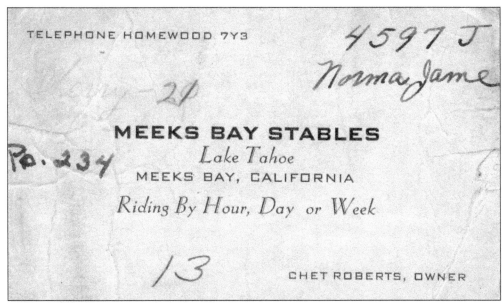

Cattleman Chet Roberts, owner of Meeks Bay Stables, grazed his cattle at Squaw Valley and higher alpine elevations. Roberts's stable was unique in having phone access for pack trips or recreational riding reservations. Please call Homewood 7Y3 for the telephone party line. (SF.)

Pack trips to the Desolation Wilderness area with its easily accessible string of lakes paralleled the Stony Ridge. Stanley "Smokey" James Samson (left) guided pack trips during the summer months from 1932 to 1938. During the summer of 1938, he led the first pack trip from Tahoe to Yosemite. The small lakes located in Desolation Wilderness offered outstanding fishing and hunting. (SF.)

Homewood has changed significantly over the years, as seen in these then (above) and now (below) images. Jake Obexer acquired property at Tahoe City and Homewood. The original shake and rough-timbered Homewood Club house has undergone significant remodeling over the years. The original building is hardly recognizable. Only the grown trees hint at its original location. The Obexer family, owners of the nearby marina, proudly celebrated the 100-year anniversary of its full service marina in Homewood in 2011. Obexer held the exclusive Union Oil Company and then Standard Oil of California petroleum products distribution franchises, converting Homewood into a sales and white-glove service hub for Gar Wood watercraft. (Both, KP.)

Four

LET'S GO TO THE BEACH

The first glimpse of Lake Tahoe, as seen from Echo Summit on Highway 50 from Sacramento, is the most anticipated moment for the first-time visitor, the seasonal tourist, and the local arriving home. Oh, how blue it is! As the 19th-century mining engineer saw the rock fissures, and the lumber baron saw the timber, so the 20th-century visitor sees the water. Lake Tahoe is an alpine lake with a maximum water level of 6,229.1 feet above sea level. It is the highest alpine lake in the United States and the largest alpine lake in North America. Best of all, the water's edge is easily accessible from both the land and the water along most of its western shore—there are no 40-feet granite boulders over which to scramble.

Visitors to Lake Tahoe quickly notice the purity of the air and are invigorated by the altitude. Unpacking the train valise or the minivan can wait while all hike to the beach. The West Shore has pebbly beaches formed from glacial action over geologic time. The sparkling blue water is inviting, but *brrrrr* is it cold! The summer surface water temperature is approximately 68 degrees Fahrenheit and drops to 47 degrees Fahrenheit at 200 feet below the surface. For those who wish to stay dry, fishing may be more enticing than swimming.

Mark Twain listed a Tahoe trout—the Lahontan cutthroat—as one of his favorite meals in *A Tramp Abroad*. Twain lamented European hotel food and included this local delicacy in his homesick fantasy menu. Fish were so abundant in the 1870s that the West Shore supported a commercial fishing industry, shipping trout at 15¢ per pound. Mackinaw trout were introduced to Tahoe in 1886 from the Great Lakes and quickly displaced Twain's treasured Lahontan cutthroat. Today, the Mackinaw trout (*Salvelinus namaycush*) is the predominate game fish in the lake. The biggest fish ever caught in Lake Tahoe, a Mackinaw trout, weighed 37 pounds, six ounces.

The first thing visitors do at the West Shore is head to the beach. Lake Tahoe has 72 miles of shoreline, and the West Shore consists mostly of sandy, pulverized-granite beaches. Off go the Victorian shirtwaists and celluloid colors. On go the black, woolen one-piece bathing suits and ladies' midi-blouse bathing dresses. These sun-loving 1911 vacationers are at Meeks Bay. (KP.)

John McKinney—mountain man, hay rancher, and cattleman—knew the West Shore as early as 1861 and moved his cattle operations to Burton Creek from Georgetown that year. By 1863, McKinney had established his 160-acre Hunters Retreat, consisting of sapling pier, log cabin, tents, and fishing boats. It is from these modest beginnings that Chamber's Landing evolved. (KP.)

58

The mountains were not replanted after logging, and 80 years after the West Shore was essentially clear-cut of its timber resources, the mountainsides are still bare. This photograph taken along Rubicon Bay in 1947 and looking north from Rubicon Point shows some original timber remaining at lakeshore. George Newhall purchased the tract, subdivided it, and sold lots in the 1960s and 1970s. (SFPL.)

This shivering little girl c. 1955 looks to be saying, "The lake is really, really cold! Hurry up and take the picture! I dare you to take the plunge." The surface water near the shore averages 68 degrees Fahrenheit all summer as snow runoff enters Tahoe from 63 creeks and leaves through only one outlet, the Truckee River. Tahoe water is 99.9 percent pure, never freezes, and gets colder farther out from the shore.

Edward Heller, son of Clara Hellman Heller and Emmanuel Heller; family friend Anis Van Nuys; and an unidentified man ride in a donkey cart along the Lake Shore c. 1910. The young boy, Edward, would become an investment banker and early founder of today's Silicon Valley. However, simple family pleasures and relaxation were the plans for the day in the early 20th century as they are today in the early 21st century at Pine Lodge. In the background is the southern boathouse so familiar to present day visitors to Sugar Pine Point. (Above, FD; below; EDCM.)

Meeks Bay's attraction was first as a summertime milk cow–grazing meadow for the Murphy brothers of Colma, California. The canyon and surrounding area was logged for its marketable timber, thereby making Meeks Creek, now a meadow, even more attractive for the Murphy brothers' cattle-grazing operation. Magulu Watah (Meeks Bay), a gathering place on ancestral Washoe land, is once more under the stewardship of the Washoe Tribe of California and Nevada. (CSL.)

The sheer drop off from Rubicon Point shown here reaches the greatest depths of Lake Tahoe. Originally formed by volcanic action, the caldera was located here, where the lake bottom is 1,645 feet below the surface. The steamer SS *Tahoe* is shown rounding the point with a recreational rower in the foreground. (KP.)

Daylong picnics at remote sites accessible by water are always a favorite. Vacationing together in 1911, these six women are in a rowing launch of the type brought to the West Shore in the late 1880s. Launches with a fringe on top and more modern versions—including pre-1900, two-cylinder steam launches and the Canadian Electric boat of this same design—are still seen today on Lake Tahoe. (KP.)

Lateen sail–rigged fishing boats disappeared with the end of commercial fishing in 1917. Powerboats were the popular watercraft for the next 50 years. Recreational sailing did not gain popularity at Lake Tahoe initially because of inconsistent winds but became a popular activity in the 1970s. This Ranger 26 named *Not to Worry*, manned by Dr. Harvey Perman and crew, raced across the lake and won the Tahoe Yacht Club–sponsored Trans Tahoe race in 1984. (HP.)

Hunting for black bear was a sport offered by guides and was often a rite of passage for young boys, like those shown here. Guide Chet Roberts (left), of Meeks Bay Stables, poses with his clients and two trophies. There is no sport bear-hunting season in Lake Tahoe California. Today, organizations like the Bear League of Homewood work to educate the public about the true nature of these animals. (NLTHS.)

Each man shown here and the cameraman bagged a six-point buck in a successful deer hunt. Sport deer hunting remains a seasonal, fall sport along the West Shore. Hunters are seen hiking into California wilderness areas west of Deer Park Springs and Five Lakes in late August through mid-October during archery and regular sport seasons. (SF.)

The Truckee River's outlet from Lake Tahoe in Tahoe City was first gated in 1870. Since then, the lake level has been artificially maintained for both downstream flood control and as the domestic water source for Reno, Nevada. The current outlet gates date from 1913. (EDCM.)

The trout fishing in the Truckee River has always been an angler's dream. The trout spawn in the lake's 63 feeder creeks, mature, and may travel for feeding downstream from the lake through the Truckee River outlet. This fly fisherwoman from the 1920s would cast today from late April to mid-November, limit her catch to two, only keep fish larger than 15 inches total length, and use only artificial lures with barbless hooks. (SFPL.)

This group of six women vacationing from San Francisco will leave their guide to the fishing duties along Blackwood Canyon. The ladies fearlessly pose on a single log while crossing the stream. Walking skirts, pigeon-front blouses, and fashionable wide-brim hats are the recreational apparel of the day in 1911. (KP.)

Some unlucky modern-day anglers may wonder whether fish can be hooked from the lakeshore. This gentleman in a Tahoe Tavern Photography Studio advertisement shows that anyone can catch trout in style at Tahoe Pines. Perhaps the suit, tie, and street shoes are the good-luck tokens or bait that attracts the fish. (CSL.)

The Lahontan cutthroat trout (also known as lake trout) is the famed gourmet fish of Lake Tahoe. These two beauties were surely eaten that night. A grilled lake trout recipe calls for two pounds of lake trout fillets, one tablespoon of lemon juice, one tablespoon of grated onion, two teaspoons of salt, and a dash of pepper. The cooking instructions are simple: clean and oil the grill. Baste and grill fish over medium-hot coals for eight minutes, turn, baste, and cook for seven minutes. Serve and enjoy. (NLTHS.)

Lake trout prepared by Tahoe Tavern chefs can be large enough to be presented with apples in their mouths. The cuisine at the tavern featured local specialties every night. (EDCM.)

This menu from Chamber's Landing during the 1950s features the popular "continental cuisine," which includes better-known entrees from Western Europe. Interestingly, the menu offers squab (young domestic pigeon) masquerading as chicken. A "New York Cut Steak"—a man's favorite— priced at $5 in 1955 would cost $42 in inflation-adjusted 2012 money. (NLTHS.)

Dinner De Luxe

Choice of One

Mixed Green Salad	Chilled Fruit Juice
Sea Food Cocktail	Fruit Cocktail
	Soup Du Jour

ENTREES

Filet of Sole Menueire	2.90
French Fried Jumbo Prawns	3.00
Eastern Scallops, French Fried, Tartar Sauce	3.00
Scaloppini of Veal, a la Marsala	3.50
Chopped Sirloin Steak with Mushroom Sauce	3.00
Breaded Veal Cutlet	3.00
Half Fried Chicken or Broiled	3.00
Roast Tom Turkey, Cramberry Sauce	3.50
Medallion of Filet with Wild Rice, Mushroom Sauce	4.50
Chicken Saute Sec with Mushrooms	3.50
Roast Prime Rib of Beef (Sat. & Sun. only)	4.00
Veal Cutlet a la Parmigiana	3.75
Chicken a la Cacciatore	3.50
Boneless Squab Chicken Stuffed with Wild Rice	4.25

FROM THE BROILER

Tenderlion Tips en Brochette (Mushrooms & Wild Rice)	4.25
Double French Lamb Chops	4.50
Filet Mignon, "THE QUEEN" of the Red Meats	5.00
Top Sirloin Steak . . . Packed with Flavor	4.50
New York Cut Steak . . . a Man's Favorite	5.00

DESSERTS

Ice Cream	Sherbert	Jello
Coffee	Tea	Milk

CHILD'S DINNER with Soup or Salad . . Half Price

Your Host FRANK L. HAVILAND   Your Chef BILL HODGES

Not Responsible For Lost Articles

Chefs at Lake Tahoe resorts are as renowned as the resorts themselves. Driven off their mining claims by the Foreign Miners Tax of 1852, most Chinese people were expelled from the mining fields by the 1860s. A job as a lumber-camp cook was one of the few jobs that Chinese people could hold in the late 1800s. By the 20th century, a Chinese cook was a source of pride. Wing Yee, longtime head chef at Homewood Resort, reflects the restaurant's pride and assurance of excellent quality food. (KP.)

Live musical entertainment was a welcome leisure at Lake Tahoe. The Walters Orchestra from San Francisco provided the August 10, 1922, dance music entertainment in Tahoe City. The tradition of summer music continues today with the annual Lake Tahoe Music Festival. (KP.)

The Carson Brewing Company (established in 1860) brewed steam beer for the thirsty Virginia City miners. Proprietor Max Stenz converted the brewery to lager in 1913 with the advent of cold storage; he named his lager Tahoe Beer with the marketing slogan, "Famous as the Lake." The pure water came not from Lake Tahoe but from King's Canyon Creek in Carson City, Nevada. Production continued until 1948 when the owner liquidated the company.

Excursion rates for fraternal or union outings brought tour groups to Tahoe. These railroad employees and their guests pose in front of the Lake Tahoe Railway & Transportation passenger cars at the Truckee depot. Notable are the railroad engineers' and firemen's clean Sunday apparel. (CRRM.)

Amateur theatrics are part of the fun at Lake Tahoe. This troupe of eight vacationing women at Homewood c. 1915 are all dressed up in caricature of their menfolk, down to the shooting irons and whiskey bottle being poured into an enamel cup. Visitors continue to enjoy seasonal theater, thanks to the Tahoe Players and the Lake Tahoe Shakespeare Festival, founded in 1972 at Sugar Pine Point State Park. (EDCM.)

These six ladies from San Francisco enjoy a barbecue at Meeks Bay, also known as Meigs Bay, Micks Bay, and Murphys Bay. The place as it is known today is named for John Meeks, an early land claimant. The Meeks brothers bailed 25 tons of wild hay in the meadows at the mouth of Meeks Creek in 1862. The Central Pacific possessed the land by the 1870s as part of its extensive US railroad grant. (KP.)

The Fleishhackers, along with their extended family and friends, motor on the *Idyllwild*, their private launch, to the remote beach in the shadow of Rubicon Point for a picnic. Fleishhacker brothers Mortimer and Herbert had long-standing investments in the region. In 1909, they held majority stock ownership of the Truckee River General Electric Company with a capital of $3 million. Their Floriston, Nevada, pulp and paper mill was the second largest in the nation. (CHS.)

The remote beach along Rubicon Bay, accessible primarily by boat, changed dramatically over the next 50 years. The same Rubicon Point location, accessible only by boat in the 1920s, is often filled to camping capacity in 2012. The private motor launches and Newhall family compound are now part of the D.L. Bliss State Park. The D.L. Bliss family donated 744 acres to the State of California in 1929. (CSL.)

The picnics and family reunions get larger as the West Shore becomes more and more accessible and popular in the post–World War II period. This extended-family picture captures the relaxation and enjoyment of good family fun and barbecue during a summer reunion at Meeks Bay Resort. Al Delclaux (left) and Jack Mauzac (right, carving a leg of lamb) enjoy the summer outing in 1959. The bocce ball competition takes place right after the marshmallow roast. (SFPL.)

These six intrepid women vacationers in the summer of 1911 wait at lake level for their ascent to Rubicon Peak. The young boy consults the map and visitor's guide. Several women display Hershey's chocolate bars for incentive or extra energy. It is a three-mile hike from the lakeshore to the top of Rubicon Peak and an elevation gain of almost 3,000 feet. (KP.)

The higher elevations surrounding Tahoe can be snow-covered for most of the year. Rock-hopping and meandering through snow caves and canyons is part of the challenge of the ascent. Incredible microclimates supporting sierra mountain daisies, clarkia, sticky monkey flowers, ferns, and snow flowers flourish in ice caverns along the way. Hikers stop here for a snack and quick energy. (KP.)

Tahoe is a land of striking contrasts. Boulder-hopping in a cool snow cave is quickly replaced with difficult hiking on loose granite scree or talus on a warm southern-exposure slope. Hiking staffs and wide straw hats help in the ascent. Cheryl Melnick is pictured with the hiking staff. (KP.)

The difficulty of the hike has its reward in an incredible view from the top of Rubicon Peak (elevation 9,183 feet). The peak is capped with a pluton on which the hikers perch. From their crow's-nest vantage, they can view the entire lake and peek over the Carson Range into Nevada. (KP.)

For many West Shore visitors, summer recreation is shopping for souvenirs. The Washoe people are noted for their outstanding basket-weaving skills. This tribesman stands on the pier and offers baskets for sale to passengers awaiting water transport back to their resorts. On the left is a truncated cone or cup (*sing-am*). Held on the right is a burden basket (*mokeewit*). (KP.)

The most famous of all the Washoe basket makers is Dat So La Le (born Dabuda, also known as Louisa Keyser), shown here with outstanding examples of her skill. Her baskets and skills were promoted and marketed by Carson City Emporium Store proprietors Abe and Amy Cohn. The Cohn Emporium secured exclusive rights to all her basket production and gave personal identity to what had been a generic product. (NLTHS.)

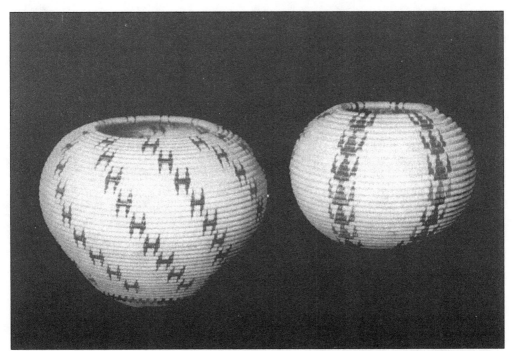

Dat So La Le is perhaps best known for her introduction of a new form of basketry known as *degikup*, as shown here. This new basket was round in form with a small opening at the top, compared to the opening in most baskets, which is the widest circumference of the item. Their sizes ranged from large (24 inches or taller) to micro (1.5 inches or smaller). (NLTHS.)

Over the course of her career, Dat So La Le created over 100 baskets, commanding a price of $1,400 for one in 1914, which would be more than $30,000 in 2012 US currency. Key to its valuation were a description ledger, certificate of authenticity, and store stickers on the bottom of each basket, initialed by the artist. The Cohns created brand identification and actively marketed the work as masterpieces in the Arts and Crafts movement. (NLTHS.)

Sept 3/06.
arrived O.K. after
a long trip. 4 hours
late. weather Perfect
had our window
open all night.
Eating is fine
& our appetites are
finer still. very
warm to-day. just
what we want. will
go fishing now.
feel fine.
Yours Milton

Mc Kinneys

Real-photo postcards personalized with the sender's remarks helped to promote tourism at Lake Tahoe. These early cards were exceedingly popular and are a major source of documentation of what small-town America looked like at the turn of the 20th century. Itinerant photographers with their cumbersome cameras captured the images and developed them on the spot for printing onto postcard stock. (KP.)

Competition to host the Panama Pacific International Exhibition (PPIE) was fierce between New Orleans, San Diego, and San Francisco. The San Francisco PPIE Commission went into overdrive, convincing Congress that San Francisco was the best choice. Lake Tahoe was an emotional extension of the city. PPIE's visit to San Francisco was emblazoned across all media. (DD.)

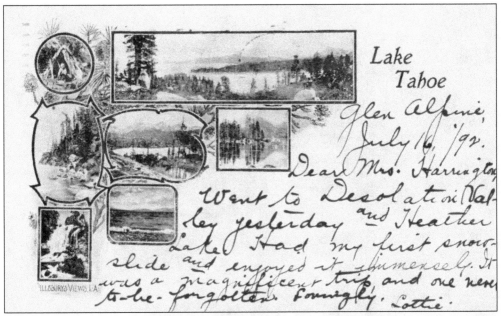

Private mailing cards were approved by the US post office on May 19, 1893, and were an immediate success. They were not technically postcards, as only the federal government was able to print the word "postcard" on the back of cards. These cards are alternatively named souvenir cards, mail cards, or correspondence cards. This card, sent in 1902 from Glen Alpine to Oakland, California, is one of the first such cards created to promote Lake Tahoe. It includes representations of, from left to right, (first row) Cascade Falls and the lakeshore; (second row) Rubicon Point, Fallen Leaf Lake, and Meeks Bay with steamer; (third row) a Washoe bark-and-pole conical shelter and Emerald Bay. Writing was allowed only on the face of the card. The undivided back was reserved for the address. This changed in 1907, allowing more area for a personal message. As a result, postcard mailing boomed, and millions of cards were published and sent at the 1¢ rate. (Both, KP.)

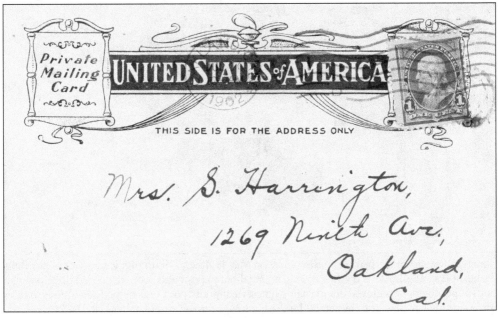

Real-photo postcards were exceedingly popular in the 1910s. This card, sent from McKinney's Hunters Retreat by Julie L. Hawley on August 7, 1910, to Emma Byne in San Francisco reads, "One of the many little bits of scenery up in the mountains. A shady trail leads thro the green meadows spangled with goldenrod & mt. daisies. I hope you had a pleasant vacation. Kindest regards & best wishes." (KP.)

Congress first authorized private mailing cards on May 19, 1898. This undivided-back card extolling the beauty of Lake Tahoe is the first of its kind. Real-photo postcards soon succeeded these popular cards as photographers moved out of their studios. Real-photo postcards helped generate cash flow while seeking the perfect commercial landscape image for the studio gallery (KP.)

Five

OVERLAND BY AUTOMOBILE

The automobile arrived at Lake Tahoe in 1910 as soon as Californians began their romance with internal combustion engines. Whether an automobile is referred to as a "tin lizzy," "flivver," "jalopy," or "doodle bug," it is a personal freedom device.

Rubicon Springs, accessible from the west on California Highway 49 from Georgetown, was a destination health resort in the early 19th century. The resort's sulfur, carbonated, and mineral springs were eagerly sought for their medicinal, curative, and restorative properties. Rubicon Springs, located less than 20 miles from the shores of Lake Tahoe, was initially as popular a destination as the shorefront resorts. Getting there involved a pack train until 1910 when the proprietors successfully brought a Maxwell over the unimproved road for the first time. Signs warned motorists of probable impassibility of the route and the extreme cost of a tow. Today's Jeepers Jamboree participants know the Georgetown-to-Tahoe route as the Rubicon Trail. In the 1920s, pioneering off-road enthusiasts drove their wide wheel-based Buick, a Maxwell, or a Studebaker to the resort.

Asphalt paving of California Highway 50 and Interstate 80 brought new meaning to the phrase, "If you build it, they will come." Successful grading of California Highway 89, connecting South Lake Tahoe to Tahoe City and Truckee, created the Wishbone Route by which motorists could drive to Lake Tahoe from Sacramento along one route and return home via the other. This enabled motorists from San Francisco to make a loop and see more of the Tahoe Basin, bringing more tourists to the West Shore. The Tahoe-Sierra Chamber of Commerce in cooperation with the Tahoe Tavern operation went into overdrive in attracting new, automobile-centric consumers. As the personal automobile supplanted train travel, more and different types of visitors gained access to the West Shore. Car camping, longer stays, and economy trips all became possible with the added mobility provided by the personal automobile.

Automobiles find their way first to Rubicon Springs in 1908. The roads are barely wagon trails. This intrepid Studebaker is on a promotional drive from Auburn to Rubicon Springs and is actually on the county road. Access to Rubicon Springs was by mule train until 1886, then by wagon for the next 20 years until advent of the automobile. (EDCM.)

Rubicon Springs proprietor Sierra Phillips Clark catered to tourists seeking the restorative qualities of the carbonated waters and the Sierra Nevada altitude. The 16-room hotel and resort spa was not on the shores of Lake Tahoe but was accessible along a one-way road from Lake Tahoe on the east via the Rubicon Road, built by the county after 1886. Prior to that, mules had provided the only transportation to the remote area. (CSL.)

The wagon roads leading into the mountains were unpaved, except by granite boulders. The way ahead could just as easily have been marked with stones piled on top of one another to create "ducks" indicating the route. The owners of the Rubicon Springs marked the road with a sign proclaiming, "Enter all cars at your own risk. Fee for towing $25." (EDCM.)

At some points, the road disappears entirely and visitors might as well have rowed a boat to the destination. The modern Jeepers Jamboree participants have nothing on these early intrepid motorists! (EDCM.)

The road along the West Shore remained unpaved and impassable in the winter up until the advent of the automobile. Commercial and private steamer craft, such as the SS *Tahoe*, *Meteor*, *Nevada*, *QUI-CH-KIDDIN*, and the *Marion B.*, continued to be the preferred method for getting around the Tahoe Basin until the late 1930s. This 1927 view of the "emerald lake" shows the treacherous one-lane road. (SFPL.)

Driving was not an experience for the faint of heart. But the opening of logging roads through remaining timber stands brought increased accessibility to the public. Which came first? The car camp or the car breakdown that necessitated overnight camping? (NLTHS.)

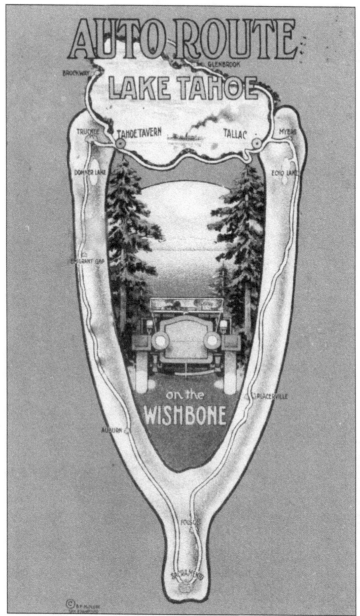

Visitors were encouraged to drive their personal automobiles to Lake Tahoe via the Wishbone Route. Improvement of the wagon road connecting Tahoe City to South Lake Tahoe in 1913 opened the West Shore to more tourism possibilities. Portions of the route were improved as a "corduroy" or "rib" route using lumber set perpendicular to the road direction. The route, anchored at Sacramento, connected the Y at South Shore with Tahoe City and Truckee to create a scenic driving loop. Extra tires, tubes, tow chains, and pumps were a necessity when travelling along this route. There were no guard rails, lines painted down the middle of the road, or call boxes. Visitors were just as likely to be stuck in the sand around Sugar Pine Point as they were to be hit by falling granite rocks. There was no need to close the gate at Emerald Bay to physically separate the West Shore from the South Shore in winter because the snow made the route impassable from late October to May every year. (DD.)

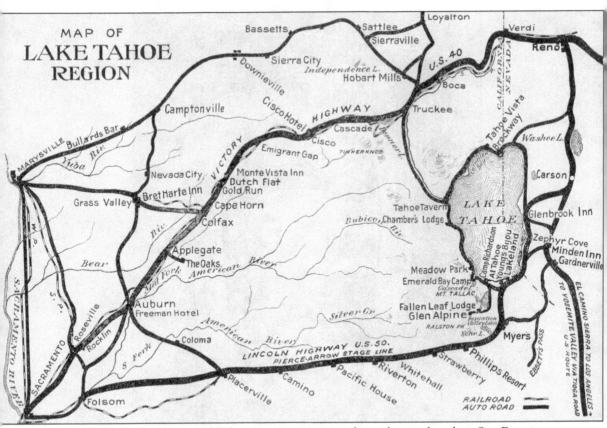

The Wishbone Route opened Tahoe to visitors coming from places other than San Francisco or who had previously been restricted to rail transportation. The Sacramento and San Joaquin valleys had a large and mobile population in California prior to World War II. It was easy work for this sizeable new population base to motor along the original Lincoln Highway over Donner Summit on Highway 40 from Sacramento to Truckee. Alternatively, a drive along the alternate Lincoln Highway route on Highway 50 to Al Tahoe or Bijou was possible once the Johnson Toll Road joined the national highway system. Adding the lakeshore road as the connection between the original (Highway 40) and alternate (Highway 50) routes was marketing magic. Many resorts along the West Shore transformed into motor lodges with garage or car camping accommodations. Gasoline was available in Homewood at Obexer's, located halfway between South Lake Tahoe and Tahoe City. The scenic route home along US 40, also known as the Liberty Highway, made the trip back to the Sacramento Valley complete. (KP.)

By the 1940s, automobiles were the standard for traveling to the lake. Train service to Tahoe City ended at the time of World War II when the tracks were pulled up for use in the war effort. The steam launches had been scuttled in the lake off of Glenbrook Point. From then on, access to Lake Tahoe was by automobile, leading to the car culture seen in this typical day at Lake Tahoe in the 1940s. (KP.)

Soon, every summer trip to the West Shore involved a drive around the lake. The 72-mile circumnavigation over oiled, wood ribbed, gravel, granite, and occasionally paved road was an anticipated one-day activity during a weeklong vacation by the 1950s. This couple driving their late-1920s Ford might have taken a week to accomplish the trip. (SFPL.)

The post–World War II prosperity brought more and more families to the West Shore. Newspaper advertisements showed pretty girls posing with a 1938 Nash Ambassador V8 parked along the shores of Lake Tahoe. In this instance, the Meeks Bay boathouse and pier provides the backdrop. Rubicon Peak is in the background. (SFPL.)

Youth rented and enjoyed riding "doodle bugs"—also known as scooters, Italian Vespas, or "putt-putts"—around the lake. Pictured in August 1947 are, from left to right, Donald Stewart, Virginia Stewart, and Irving and Helen Kaiser riding tandem. At one time, no driver's license was required to operate these motor bikes. Notable is the lack of safety equipment or helmets as these four circle the lake. (SFPL.)

Six

ROWING, RACING, AND YACHTING

Once visitors arrived at the lake, they could feed their love of freedom with a boat. As quickly as personal vehicles arrived on the West Shore, personal watercrafts were launched. Powerboats built by Gar Wood, Chris Craft, Century, Besotes Bros., and others became popular; today, they are generically called "woodies." Following the woodies in the 1950s were powerboats constructed of fiberglass, which often took on design elements of luxury and affordable automobiles. Often, the console of a Chevrolet or Cadillac became the instrument panel of a powerboat. The design element of a "boat tail" could just as easily be found on 1932 Duesenberg or 1935 Auburn boattail speedsters as on a powerboat's stern. The key to the wooden boat experience, however, is the engine. Large Scripps, Lycoming, or Gray V-12 engines were necessary to move a mahogany craft, often weighing more than two tons. Nothing is more exhilarating than a 28-foot, triple-cockpit Gar Wood speeding with bow heeling out of the water. Better yet, an aircraft engine could be put in an aluminum, flat-bottomed speedboat and a water speed record attempted. Tahoe's West Shore has been the home of chauffeur-driven, matronly vessels and world-water-speed-record challenges.

Jake Obexer first secured the Union and the Standard Oil petroleum product rights for the West Shore in early 1913. His Tahoe City distributorship provided gas and oil products year-round for both the automobile engine and the woodie engine. Which came first to Tahoe—the gasoline for the car or the petrol for the boat? The increased number of personal automobiles coming to Tahoe and the number of pleasure boats on the lake drove demand for energy. By the 1930s, Obexer secured the Gar Wood dealership for his new focus of operations on the West Shore, Homewood. Personal watercraft ownership and rental made water sports available to all visitors.

The Tahoe Powerboat Club, later renamed the Tahoe Yacht Club, was founded in 1925 to provide a social group focused on the love of boating for summer residents. Founding members Henry J. Kaiser (shipyard owner and industrialist) and Robert S. Dollar (shipping magnate and lumber baron) both enjoyed summer homes at Lake Tahoe. They and their families good-naturedly raced their powerboats and spent the off-season on the construction of more competitive or innovative speedboats. Yacht club picnics, speedboat races, and today's world-famous Concours d'Elegance, featuring classic wooden boats, evolved from these early boating diversions.

Almost as soon as the internal combustion engine provided the propulsion for automobiles, the engines were put in pleasure boats. The *Florence M II*, built at the Stephens Brothers Boat Builders (1902–1987) in Stockton, California, was destined for Lake Tahoe. The Stephens brothers were experienced builders of fast California Delta boats used by agricultural product brokers to outpace their competitors to the San Francisco commodity market. During their time, the Stephens brothers built over 1,200 speedboats, pleasure boats, cruisers, and yachts. The *Florence M II* was a 26-feet, double-cockpit, runabout with an internal engine amidships. She was built in 1926 at the boat works for Elliott F. Morse and named for his daughter Florence and M for Morse. Florence married J. Carroll Skinner, who was a pre–World War II commodore of the Lake Tahoe Powerboat Club. The *Florence M II* was only one of 11 boats built at the Stephens' boat works that was delivered to Lake Tahoe for pleasure use. Morse, his daughter Florence, and granddaughter Marilyn Bewley piloted this boat for nine decades of Stephens' races and afternoon rides on the lake. (TMM.)

The plucky REO Motoring Company touring car (1917 design) successfully pulled the *Florence M II* across the Sacramento Valley and through the Mother Lode. The boat with trailer is longer and heavier than the automobile. Ascending the Sierra Nevada is another matter. Transporting the boat to Tahoe over State Highway 50, the Johnson Toll Road, and over Ebbett's Pass (elevation 8,730 feet) required double-teaming of vehicles. (TMM.)

Not surprisingly, it is a lot easier going downhill. Instead of relying on the brakes, it was necessary to put the REO in low gear and take the occasion to enjoy the route. The 350-mile trip took two days. The touring car ran on kerosene as converted from gas during World War I. The craft is transported on a farm wagon chassis with no auxiliary brakes on the trailer. (TMM.)

The REO and *Florence M II* arrive at the Lake with a story to tell. The touring car and runabout are still telling their story today. The fully restored automobile, trailer, and boat are maintained in first-class running condition by the Tahoe Maritime Museum. This wonderful museum and living history organization keeps the West Shore's love of classic automobiles and vintage pleasure craft alive at their Homewood and Truckee locations. (TMM.)

The *Florence M II* is launched from the beach at Al Tahoe in 1925. Everyone lends a hand—owner, man, woman, and child—in rolling the trailer down to the water's edge. Why not back the boat trailer down to the lake with the REO motor car? Those narrow wheels mire down in the sand or snow and gain no traction. (TMM.)

J.P. "Jake" Obexer purchased property at Homewood in 1922. In 1930, Obexer had acquired the Lake Tahoe franchise rights for Gar Wood watercraft. Those West Shore residents who weathered the Depression purchased powerboats during the 1930s. Obexer both maintained the beautiful mahogany-and-steel watercraft and sold the petroleum and the oil products to propel them. A triple cockpit Gar Wood would fly with a Scripps V-12 motor. (TMM.)

The Tahoe Yacht Club offered social occasions for good-natured competition among powerboat owners. Several of these boats have continued in family ownership and can still be viewed traveling over Lake Tahoe today. The distractive sound and pitch of the wood boat speeding at full throttle is hard to miss. The Tahoe Yacht Club continues the tradition by sponsoring the annual Concours d'Elegance in August. (TMM.)

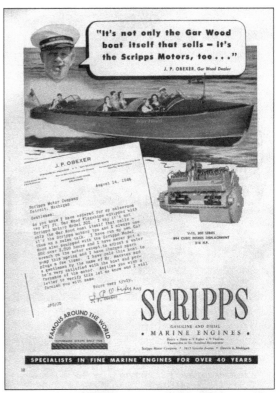

The Gar Wood boating legend traces its roots to New York and Michigan with a series of boatyards, designs, and American powerboat racing successes in the 1920s. The *Apache I*, later renamed *Miss San Francisco* and then the *Tecolote II*, was a Hacker Boat Company, New York, design. Hacker and Gar Wood were the pre– and post–World War II gold standard for pleasure boating and racing. (NLTHS.)

Powerboats of all descriptions were available for all budgets. Many people owned an outboard motor and rented a boat for $5 a day for pleasure, fishing, or water skiing. The introduction of fiberglass boats in the 1950s made boating economical because these boats required minimal maintenance compared to the traditional or wooden boats.

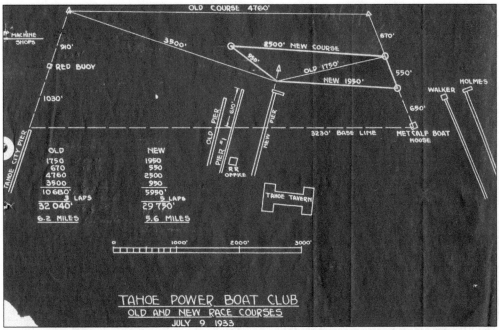

Powerboat races were held near Tahoe City in the 1930s for optimum shore viewing. Not surprisingly, the best viewing was from the Tahoe Tavern. Later, a second and six-mile course was added near Chamber's Landing for a second weekend of summer races. In the 1950s and 1960s, nationally sanctioned Unlimited-class thunder boat racing became a popular annual event. (TMM.)

The *Hornet II*, a stepped-hull hydroplane (hull built by Gar Wood in 1930), is powered by a 600-horsepower engine. Driven by Henry Kaiser Sr., it flies by spectators during the 1939 powerboat races. Kaiser, in competition with Stanley Dollar Jr. and his *Mercury* and *Baby Skipalong*, won many races over the years. The boat is a regular favorite at the annual Lake Tahoe Concours d'Elegance classic boat show. (NLTHS.)

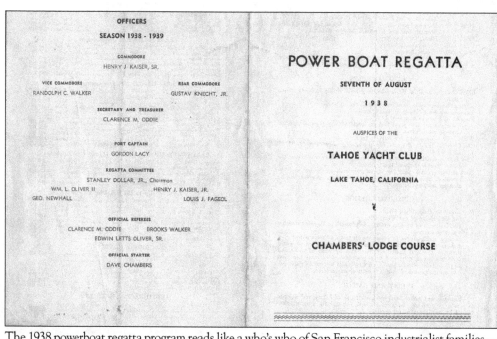

The 1938 powerboat regatta program reads like a who's who of San Francisco industrialist families—fathers and sons with an occasional wife or widow. It is this year that the Lake Tahoe Powerboat Club changed its name to the Lake Tahoe Yacht Club. Participants included Henry Kaiser Sr., Kaiser Shipyards and Kaiser Sand and Gravel; Henry Kaiser Jr., Kaiser Steel and Kaiser Motors; R. Stanley Dollar Sr. and R. Stanley Dollar Jr., Dollar Steamship Lines; Walter Heller, San Francisco investment banker; Herbert Fleishhacker Jr., Crocker-Anglo National Bank; George Pope, lumber and shipping; B. Charles Ehrman, banking; Lora J. Knight, a financial backer of Lindbergh's Atlantic flight and owner of Vikingsholm, Emerald Bay; Mrs. Claude (Ester) Lazard, French banking firm Lazard Freres and heir to Pine Lodge, Sugar Pine Point; Ruth (husband Dick) Shainwald, cousins of the Walter Heller family; Randolph C. Walker, president of Aireon Manufacturing Company (aircraft accessories, airplane radios, and jukeboxes), and others. (Both, TMM.)

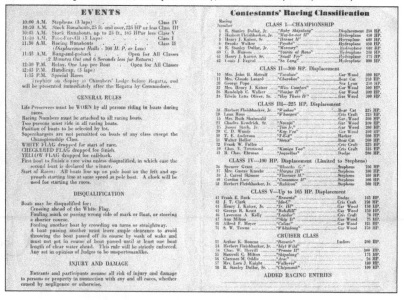

Local sportsman Stanley Dollar Jr. (1915–1975) pilots the wooden boat *Baby Skipalong*, formerly the *Greenwich Folly*. The craft won the Lake Tahoe Yacht Club speedboat championship in 1936 but lost to Herbert Fleishhacker, driving *May-be-not II*, in 1938. (TMM.)

In 1937, Stanley Dollar Jr. purchased the 35-foot aluminum speedboat *Cigarette IV*, built in 1926, and renamed her *Mercury*. She was one of the fastest speedboats ever built. *Mercury*, with its 600-horsepower, Curtis D-12 engine, still runs on the lake today. She can be heard for miles and is on display at the south boathouse at Ed Z'berg Sugar Pine Point where she can still be admired. (TMM.)

Local favorite Stanley Dollar Jr. poses for a publicity shot with Barbara Swain atop Dollar's hydroplane entry the *Short Snorter* on September 2, 1954. Dollar began his love for speed as a young man and never tired of the competition. A decorated World War II veteran, Dollar continued his interest in the big aircraft engine–powered thunder boats until his death in 1975. (TMM.)

Sky High hydroplane races featured the largest unlimited-class boats. Drivers Kenny St. Oegger in Henry Kaiser's *Hawaii Kai* and Jay Murphy in *Breathless U-22* (shown here) dueled for Lake Tahoe's Mapes Cup in 1958. Tahoe was a stop for the unlimited-class hydroplane race tour from 1962 to 1965, and the Lake Tahoe Yacht Club's flag was on the tail fins of some of these boats. (NLTHS.)

Hydroplanes are designed to ride on a cushion of air with often only their propeller in the water. Air is trapped under the hull allowing minimum friction and for the craft to literally fly. The C-class hydroplanes must be at least 11 feet and six inches long with a minimum weight of 440 pounds. They are designed to carry medium-to-heavy-weight drivers. (TMM.)

In 1938, Henry J. Kaiser (right) displays the much-coveted Lake Tahoe Yacht Club Commodore's Powerboat Racing Cup, which would be awarded to the regatta winner. These awards are still part of club memorabilia and can be admired at the Tahoe Yacht Club offices in Tahoe City. (NLTHS.)

Father and son admire a pusher floatplane (seaplane) as it lifts off from Tahoe during the July 1958 Mapes Cup hydroplane races. Notable is the direction of the propellers on this aluminum amphibian aircraft. (SFPL.)

Miss Lake Tahoe 1962 (wearing gloves and a corsage), with her court of runners-up, is welcomed in South Lake Tahoe airport on arrival on Tahoe Airlines. Beauty pageants were very popular with the powerboat racing set in the 1950s and 1960s. Miss Lake Tahoe would have competed later that year in the Miss Nevada pageant. She and her royal court are escorted by a VFW representative (left) and chamber of commerce representative (right). (KP.)

Seven

RELIGIOUS AND CINEMATIC OUTREACH

Private automobiles improved access to Lake Tahoe, and more visitors arrived every season. How best could the Tahoe experience be shared with those who had not yet traveled to the "magical West Shore?" Communicating the beauty, delight, and restorative qualities of Lake Tahoe's West Shore was limited to word of mouth, printed matter, and images until the advent of the silent movie era. Private mailing cards and real-photo postcards told the West Shore story from the 1880s to 1910s. Access was easiest during the summer months when visitors took the Central Pacific railroad to Truckee, transferred to narrow gauge locomotive to travel to Tahoe City, and took steamer launch to their final West Shore destinations.

Many religious groups have incorporated the transcendental tradition in the establishment of religious camps and summer retreats in areas of extraordinary beauty, including Lake Tahoe. The Methodists created a camp at Forest Hill outside of Tahoe City, and the Episcopal Church built a fresh-air chapel on part of the original Tahoe Tavern property.

The log cabin that was occupied by Sr. Aimee Semple McPherson while establishing the Tahoe-Cedars project, her summer religious tract, is legendary in the Tahoma area. Sister Aimee was the charismatic, evangelical founder of the Foursquare Church located in Los Angeles. Developer H.L. Henry secured the Tahoe-Cedars property in Tahoma and divided it into lots for sale. The subdivision included nearly 1,000 lots; streets were laid out, power lines run, and a water system installed. Regrettably, the lot sales to church congregants were minimal, and the religious project was cancelled. The subdivision was subsequently refocused as a motion picture colony. Some of the original Tahoe-Cedars tract property owners were Lon Chaney, Lina Basquette, ballet master Ernest Belcher, and writer Francis Rawling Illes.

The movies provided outreach to a larger audience who would certainly add Tahoe to their annual holiday, religious retreat, or vacation plans. Breathtaking images, romantic scenarios, and favorite occasions could be enjoyed with the backdrop of Lake Tahoe. After watching their favorite Tahoe films, children would be begging, "Oh, Ma, can we go there next summer?" Those in need of a quick escape to the lake can rescreen *Indian Love Call*, which was also released in Europe as *Rose Marie*. Europeans responded to the imagery, opening up a new post–World War II visitors market. Seeing Tahoe on the screen is almost as good as being there.

Aimee Semple McPherson (1890–1944), the charismatic evangelical pastor, brought 5,000 of her Los Angeles followers on vacation to Tahoe-Cedars from July 15 to July 30, 1928. The Tahoe Foursquare Camp evolved from an offer by the owner of the property to donate four lots for a Lighthouse church and ministry residences. This log cabin is believed to be the pastoral house used by Sister Aimee in 1928.

The chamber of commerce, Southern Pacific Railroad, and local businesses welcomed the combined vacation park and religious revival concept. Accommodations were primarily tent camps, but there were real estate lots available for sale at the Tahoe-Cedars Christian Colony. Lots measuring 50 feet by 125 feet were available for $10–$52.50 a month (number of months not indicated). For $400, a cabin would be constructed in four days. (FSC.)

Sister Aimee, pictured here in recreational attire, planned a two-week restful vacation at Lake Tahoe. Word got out, and it was soon a full-scale camp meeting. Sister Aimee welcomed the change and quipped that she "only had to preach 2 times a day and the rest of the time she had on her own to fish (for souls)." (FSC.)

Members of the Foursquare Church remember Sister Aimee best as a charismatic pastor. She opened the doors of Angelus Temple in Los Angeles in 1923 and developed an extensive social ministry, feeding more than 1.5 million people during the Great Depression. She summarized her spiritual message into four major points, which she called the Foursquare Gospel. The Angelus Temple and affiliated Foursquare Churches continue to spread the gospel throughout the world to this day. (FSC.)

Buster Keaton (1895–1966) used the Tahoe Truckee area frequently as a site for both winter and summer sets. *The Frozen North* (1922) and *The Navigator* (1924) were both filmed here. *Our Hospitality* was filmed along the Truckee River in 1926. The Tahoe backdrop stood in for the Appalachian Mountains of Kentucky in the antebellum-themed rendition of the Hatfields-versus-the-McCoys rivalry.

This romantic location along the Truckee River could double as a film location. These two are lost in their own world. Surely, there is little fishing going on—and the lady's parasol is about to escape. (NLTHS.)

A Place in the Sun was filmed in 1951 at locations all over the West Shore and Echo Lakes. The film's stars were Montgomery Clift, Elizabeth Taylor, and Shelly Winters with Raymond Burr in a supporting role.

Elizabeth Taylor and Montgomery Clift take a moment from filming to enjoy the West Shore. Try as the author might, the location of this spot along the West Shore evades identification. Readers can win undying gratitude by e-mailing the author with the answer: cajensen@pacbell.com.

Perhaps the most famous film of its time, *Indian Love Call* was filmed on the West Shore in 1936 and was released as *Rose Marie* outside of the United States. It was filmed throughout the West Shore with the main scenes recorded at Emerald Bay. For years, this film was played every week during the summer season at the Meeks Bay movie house.

The filming of *Rose Marie* was a boon to the Washoe Nation. At the summer filming in the heart of the Depression, every Washoe who wanted a job worked as an acting extra. Tribe chief Captain Pete donned a Sioux warbonnet and portrayed a Native American from Yukon Territory, Canada. The cross-tribal dressing made no sense, but it played big in Hollywood. (NLTHS.)

Classically trained baritone Nelson Eddy (1901–1967) plays *Rose Marie*'s hero Sergeant Bruce, a Royal Canadian Mounted Police member. He and costar Jeannette MacDonald were at the height of their popularity as "America's Singing Sweethearts" when this film was released in the middle of the Great Depression. The supporting cast is rounded out with soon-to-be major stars Jimmy Stewart, Allan Jones, and David Niven.

Known for her operatic soprano voice, Jeannette MacDonald (1903–1965) played the Mountie's love interest Marie de Flor (Rose Marie). Their famous duet "The Indian Love Call" (also known as "When I'm Calling You") was the biggest hit of the movie. Eddy and MacDonald made this song their staple duet for the next two decades. The two were inducted into the Grammy Hall of Fame in 2008 on this song's merits alone. The original single sold over a million copies.

The West Shore estate known as Fleur du Lac was created in 1938 for Henry J. Kaiser and the heads of the five companies that created the Hoover Dam. The 15-acre property is staged as the Corleone compound during the 1973 filming of *The Godfather Part II* by Francis Ford Coppola. It is recognizable in both the wedding and the horse-head scenes of the film.

Fleur du Lac is featured as the Corleone estate in *The Godfather Part II*. It is the location where Don Vito Corleone's son Fredo gets "whacked." The original *Godfather* cast members are superstars. From left to right are James Caan as Sonny, Marlon Brando as Don Vito, Al Pacino as Michael, and John Cazale as Fredo.

Eight

WINTER WONDERLAND AND OLYMPIC DREAMS

It took generations to overcome the historic memory of the "Tragedy in the Sierra," as experienced by the ill-fated Donner Party at Truckee Meadows in the winter of 1846–1847. Winter in the Sierra was to be avoided if not feared. Snow playing, tobogganing, and sleighing were not for the faint of heart. Norwegian snowshoeing (skiing) was perhaps best left to Placerville mail carrier John A. "Snowshoe" Thompson. Tahoe's West Shore was a summer-season recreational retreat until *Truckee Republican Newsletter* editor Charles McGlashan and similar-minded chamber of commerce boosters mounted a campaign to attract tourists to the Truckee "ice palace," ice rink, and other snow-park amenities. Tourists arrived by train for a weekend of snow play with the promise from local hotels of warmth and safety at the end of the day.

Winter sports came to the West Shore in 1924 as the Tahoe Tavern expanded its offering to year-round accommodations and recreation. Following the success of Truckee's Ski Hill, built in 1910, Tahoe Tavern opened a ski resort in 1924 and expanded over the next 10 years. Located on the perimeter of the Tahoe Tavern property, the resort centered on a 60-feet ski jump designed by Norwegian national champion Lars Haugen in hopes of drawing both local and tourist visitors. The snow-play area was accessed by horse-drawn snow sleigh. A toboggan run and lift were soon added. The local Lake Tahoe Ski Club, founded in 1929, called Olympic Hill its home course and held competitions against other Sierra Nevada ski clubs there.

The US Ski Championships were held at Tahoe Tavern in February 1932, but the full development of a recreational ski resort in the Tahoe Basin did not materialize until after World War II. The winter ski resort is known today in its current life as Granlibakken Conference Center & Lodge after a Norwegian word that translates loosely as "a hillside sheltered by fir trees." Tahoe's dreams of hosting the Winter Olympic Games, which were first held in Chamonix, France, in 1924, were realized in February 1960 when the VII Olympic Winter Games came to Squaw Valley.

Each year's winter snowfall ended the economic life of the West Shore until 1924. Annual snowfall averages 18 feet at lake level, and temperatures can range between a low of 16 degrees Fahrenheit and a high of 40 degrees Fahrenheit during the four months of winter. Locals engaged in winter sports and entertainments, but few tourists ventured to Tahoe City during these stormy months. All of that changed when the Tahoe Tavern opened for winter guests in 1924. (KP.)

Snowfall meant shoveling to extract the small Tahoe Railroad locomotives from the drifts. The original railroad tracks extended along today's Tahoe City Commons Beach to the commercial wharf. Snow from the steeply pitched Tahoe Mercantile roof almost avalanches the locomotive. Lake Tahoe is seen in the distance. (RRM.)

The diminutive size of narrow gauge Central Pacific locomotive No. 1 C.P. *Huntingdon* is compared to the standard Southern Pacific Line's mountain-duty engine of 1922. The Southern Pacific engines were often doubled to scale the Sierra Nevada range. The Southern Pacific replaced the narrow gauge tracks in 1926, renaming their transcontinental Overland Route the Lake Tahoe Route as a promotional effort to regain passengers. (SFPL.)

TRUCKEE RIVER
REACHED BY SOUTHERN PACIFIC

In 1932, Southern Pacific began offering its "Snowball Special," a scenic trip along the Truckee River en route to the Tahoe Tavern in Pullman sleepers from the Oakland Mole. A ferryboat transportation hub is traveling alongside the train, and dogs pull a sled in training for the annual Truckee/Tahoe equivalent of the famous Alaska Iditarod sled race. Dogsled races were a popular event in Tahoe, drawing visitors from the Bay Area for a winter break. (EDCM.)

Ted Kent (shown with lead dog Blackie) was the constant winner of sled team races. Kent and his team of eight Labrador-mix dogs won at least eight dog team races in the 1920s. In February 1929, he competed in the 90-mile Sierra Dog Derby at North Lake Tahoe for a $9,000 prize, the equivalent of $118,800 in inflation-adjusted 2012 money. The eight-dog teams competed over three days in the midwinter spectator sport. (KP).

Ice sculpture and snowman building are part of the joys of winter at Tahoe. This fanciful menagerie of a snowman, dragon, stag, and camel lasted months to ornament and delight visitors to Olympic Hill and the tavern snow-play areas. (DD.)

Henry J. Kaiser and five other company presidents acquired 15 lakefront acres and built several houses and outbuildings of their Fleur du Lac compound during the summer of 1938. The main building and boathouse were erected right on the lake. That posed a significant flooding problem the following spring as the snow melted and the lake level rose. The solution was to construct a rock retaining wall to act as a dike against high water. (NLTHS.)

Some intrepid winter sports enthusiasts will make their way down the West Shore no matter the conditions. Snow drifts of 20 or more feet covering the Hut and cottages make travel along the West Shore and its roads all but impossible. Drivers and their cars find a way through in this 1930s view. (JH.)

The Lake Tahoe Ski Club formed in 1929, comprised primarily of local high school boys. To this day, the club has had more national champions and Olympians than any other ski club in America. Gone is the single ski pole used by "Snowshoe" Thompson in his treks from Placerville, California, to Genoa, Nevada, in the 1850s. The ski and binding designs would remain much the same into the 1970s. (NLTHS.)

The ski jump at Olympic Hill, Tahoe Tavern (above), opened in 1924 for the pleasure of local ski enthusiasts. This ski jump became part of Granlibakken Ski Resort and was selected by the US Olympic Committee as the location for the February 1931 Olympic trials. Reno competitor Wayne Poulsen, the future Squaw Valley developer, placed third in the ski jumping event. Although Tahoe Tavern opened in 1924, it was not until 1928 that the lodge stayed open for winter and attracted tourists to enjoy winter sports. Promotional pictures (right) emphasizing the ski jump brought jumpers and spectators. Tahoe Tavern's automobile garage was turned into an ice rink. A toboggan run was built at a site above today's Tahoe City Golf Course. Snow activities, including the toboggan run, were eventually moved to a more sheltered hill at today's Granlibakken. (Above, NLTHS; right, KP.)

TAHOE TAVERN

LAKE TAHOE, CALIFORNIA

Recreational skiing as a commercial venture slowly caught on after World War II and gained impetus into the mid-1950s. Tahoe Tavern continued its promotion of snow sports. Bill Bechdolt established a 1,300-feet-long rope tow at Tahoe City in 1936. Granlibakken was the only major ski area on the West Shore until Squaw Valley began its efforts to bring the 1960 Winter Olympics to the area. (KP.)

Summer and winter sports combine on the Truckee River with spring skiing in 1938 and early fly-fishing for trout. The Tahoe Sierra Association and local chamber of commerce did their best to bring visitors and tourist dollars to the West Shore by attracting sports enthusiasts year round. (SFPL.)

Visiting snow-play areas for tobogganing, building snowmen, launching snowball fights, or just a scenic outing was a popular recreation activity in the 1920s. Automobiles were chaining their tires and daring to face the elements. Engaged at the time, Dorothy and Rasmus Jensen stop to enjoy the moment on a warm, 1928 spring day.

Skiing was not for everyone, but snow play and ice-skating were. Members of the Lake Tahoe Ski Club take a moment to play on the Truckee River. Ice skates could be rented and clamped onto shoes with a tightening key or attached to special shoes with nails. Calf-length summer hiking boots are doing double duty for winter ice-skating. (NLTHS.)

To Wish You A Merry Christmas

LAKE TAHOE

The steamship *Meteor* rounds Rubicon Point in winter in this lovely Christmas greeting card from Lake Tahoe. The *Meteor* assumed the mail delivery, passenger, and freight duties of the SS *Tahoe* during the winter months. People along the West Shore essentially would have been snowbound for most of the winter. Only the railroad and the steamships ensured communication as required by the US mail contract. (KP.)

Travelers await the snowplow and enjoy a sunny moment in downtown Tahoe City in the 1930s. Ladies in mink and fox coats chat, skiers make for après-ski toddies, and a snappily dressed man wonders whether Baby Face Nelson really was at the Tahoe Inn last night. (KP.)

Nine

VISION FOR THE FUTURE

Americans have a long, emotional relationship with natural beauty. Transcendentalist writers Ralph Waldo Emerson (1803–1882), Henry David Thoreau (1817–1862), and Walt Whitman (1819–1892) linked the natural world with the spiritual life. Early-20th-century writer George Wharton James (1858–1923) continued in this tradition and carried this literary standard into the Arts and Crafts movement in California.

Known for its crystalline waters and healthful air, Lake Tahoe becomes a natural metaphor for spirituality, human integration with nature, and the national passion to save unparalleled sites of beauty. Pres. Abraham Lincoln signed legislation granting the Yosemite Valley and the Mariposa Grove to the State of California for protection in 1864. John Muir helped spark creation of Yosemite National Park in 1890. Pres. William McKinley proclaimed the Lake Tahoe Forest Preserve on April 13, 1899, in "an act to repeal timber-culture laws," putting 69,000 acres under public reservation. His successor Pres. Theodore Roosevelt added additional lands and renamed the Tahoe Forest Reserve on October 3, 1905, thus beginning the US National Forest System. The reserve acreage expanded to more than 870,000 acres with one pen stroke.

Today, numerous government agencies and environmental nonprofits work to ensure Lake Tahoe's continued health and beauty into the 22nd century and beyond. The League to Save Lake Tahoe, established in 1957 and focusing on water quality, was created in partial response to University of California, Davis (UC Davis) monitoring and research into lake clarity. The organization celebrates over 50 years of urging public officials to do what is best for the lake in the long term. Annual efforts, such as the Lake Tahoe Summit, sponsored by the Tahoe Fund and hosted by Sen. Dianne Feinstein, attract political attention to the relationship between lake clarity and forest health. California State Parks and Recreation, Lahontan Regional Water Quality Control Board, and nonprofits are solution oriented. Most recently, organizations, such as Friends of the West Shore, are responding to redevelopment proposals with close civic, economic, and environmental oversight.

As it was in 1880, the outstanding question today is how to balance the wide variety of natural resource uses in the Tahoe Basin to ensure a healthy local economy, employment, recreational opportunities, enjoyment of Tahoe's natural beauty, and preservation of the lake and surrounding forest.

Author George Wharton James (1858–1923) was a prolific writer and lecturer on California and the Southwest. He was a frequent visitor to Tahoe and had many friends here. His enthusiasm for the romanticism of the West, Native American crafts, and nature made him the literary heir to the transcendentalists. His Tahoe writings spurred interest in Lake Tahoe as a natural, spiritual resource. (BANC.)

The Lake of the Sky: Lake Tahoe is perhaps James's most famous work. The author's close affinity with Tahoe City is revealed in his dedication of the book to his friend Constable Robert M. Watson. This first-edition printing was published by James F. Tapley in New York in 1915. Its cover design, a distinctive Arts and Crafts motif on green cloth board, is highly collectable. The book has never gone out of print in 95 years of publication. (CD.)

Destructive and unprofitable mining on a limited scale was reactivated during the 1930s on Tahoe's West Shore. The Tahoe Treasure Mine (established in 1934) and the Noonchester Mine (established around 1932) were located a quarter of a mile south of Quail Lake near Homewood. The gold-bearing ledge was "peacock" ore, the hardest rock to mine and very costly to mill. There are remains of two mineshafts at Noonchester Mine, suggesting hard rock, not placer mining. (NLTHS.)

Residential construction boomed in the 1960s with developments promoted by Newhall from Rubicon on the south to Hurricane Bay nearing Tahoe City on the north. Developers and real estate agents dramatically promoted the custom homes constructed for vacation or seasonal use. Construction employment was added to tourism as a major source of employment in the area. (CHS.)

Interest in the lake's geological and anthropological past was sparked with the occasional washing up on shore of dugout canoes, the discovery of ancient tree stumps, and the reaction to reduced lake water clarity. Paul Simpson, California Department of Water Resources engineer, and his three-and-a-half-year-old son, Beaver, measure stumps up to three feet in diameter, displaying as many as 250 tree rings. This father-and-son team investigates ancient tree stumps revealed during a time of unusually low lake levels in 1961. UC Davis has taken the lead in Lake Tahoe research, beginning with the work of Dr. Charles Goldman in 1959 and continuing today with the Tahoe Environmental Research Center (TERC) in Incline Village. (SFPL.)

The future prospects of the Washoe Nation were unclear as Chief "Captain" Pete and basket maker Agnes pose for the camera in the 1930s. Native Americans were increasingly marginalized as individuals either assimilated into Euro-American culture or were left behind. Basket weaving, domestic service, field labor, and government subsidies became more and more their lot. (NLTHS.)

Visitors and locals had reason to cry as the Tahoe Tavern was slated for demolition in the 1960s. Dedicated rail and steam transportation ensured its success from 1901 through the 1920s, the Depression, and World War II, but easy automobile access sealed its fate. Years of declining patronage resulted in an auction of all furniture and fixtures. The hotel succumbed to fire in 1964, and the charred remains were demolished and removed. (NLTHS.)

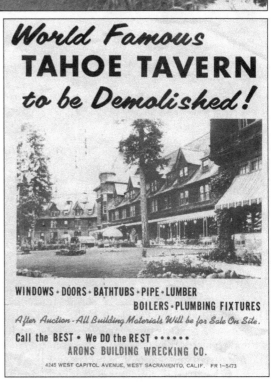

Lake Tahoe's water level was artificially changed by man with the construction of a dam on the Truckee River in Tahoe City, and a fish hatchery was created near the lake outlet. The initial dam was a wooden affair with minimal impact on Truckee River flow. Today, the City of Reno controls the top six surface feet of the lake, influencing commerce in Tahoe, Truckee, and Reno and the availability of residential housing permits in Reno. (EDCM.)

The controlling of the lake level at the Truckee River outlet at Tahoe City has continued over the years with construction of progressively newer, higher, and more sophisticated dams. The City of Reno regulates the lake level today from its Truckee River Control Center in Reno, Nevada. The pedestrian and automobile bridge over the Truckee River is colloquially and affectionately known to local Tahoe residents as "Fanny Bridge."

The Homewood Ski area has its beginning in a towrope installed in 1961 by Ron Rupp and others. Homewood Hotel and Ski Hill and the Tahoe Ski Bowl provided "old Tahoe" skiing for locals, beginners, and those seeking a relaxed ski experience. In 1987, the two ski areas were purchased by Helen Alrich and combined into the Homewood Ski Resort (above). The property has subsequently changed hands several times. The latest plan is to transform 25 acres of the property into Homewood Village Resort (artist's rendering below). The developers propose an alpine village with commercial space and high-density housing of more than 350 townhouse and hotel units with a total of more than 690 bedrooms. Conservation proponents, grassroots organizations, concerned residents, and community groups, such as the Friends of the West Shore, are monitoring public planning hearings very carefully. (Both, TIR.)

The League to Save Lake Tahoe, familiar to visitors by its ubiquitous blue sticker proclaiming, "Keep Tahoe Blue," has been safeguarding the natural beauty of the Tahoe Basin and the lake's clarity since 1957. This original postcard (above) with its message harkens back to George Wharton James's prose. The message evolved into the iconic "Keep Tahoe Blue" sticker (below) that is found on almost every SUV returning from a Tahoe vacation today. This logo has been synonymous with the league for over 40 years, and the league has produced stickers in Spanish (*Mantegna Tahoe Azul*) and Russian (*Сохрани Тахо Чистым*) in recent years. The league conducts extensive outreach and education on the environmental challenges facing Lake Tahoe. It encourages stewardship and the environmental ethic. (Above, KP.)

LAKE TAHOE

Nature may be making a comeback. UC Davis reports that water clarity has remained steady but has not reversed from 2000 to 2009. The California brown bear has made a comeback after being all but hunted to elimination in the Tahoe Basin. "Be Bear Aware" has become the new mantra as stressed and hungry bears face off with stressed and terrified homeowners over property rights.

Tahoe

God took a gem of great beauty,
Wondrous, clear, sparkling and cool:
He made, with the hands of a genius,
A set for this opalized pool.

High on the top of a mountain,
He moulded the rim with great care,
Then put the water of Tahoe,
Placed so his subjects might share.

He gilded the peaks with sunset,
With moonlight, burnished the wave—
Wove in the hues of the rainbow,
Remember—He promised to save.

A. Allen Stafford.

The League to Save Lake Tahoe and the North Lake Tahoe Historical Society urge visitors to do their parts to save Lake Tahoe and continue its historic legacy.

West Shore Resorts

The following is a list of past and present Lake Tahoe resorts and campgrounds located along the Lincoln Highway (California State Highway 89) from Tahoe City to Rubicon Point along the West Shore, except where noted.

Tahoe House
Tahoe Inn
Tahoe Tavern
Waleswood Lodge
Valentines Cottages
Schlueter's
Tahoe Park
Nicholson's
Pomin's Tahoe Park
Worden's Camp
Tahoe Lodge
William Kent Camp Ground
Sunnyside
Tahoe Pines
Fleur du Lac
Cedar Crest
Willowwood Camp and the Hut
Homewood Resort
El Campo
Chamber's Lodge

McKinney's Hunters Retreat
Rubicon Springs (Up McKinney Creek and west)
Pine Crest
Edward's Cottages
Tahoma
Tahoe Cedar Lodge
Gregory's Cottages
Moana Villa
Pomin's Lodge
Fanger's Lodge
Bellevue Hotel (within present Ed Z'berg Sugar
   Pine Point State Park)
Ed Z'berg Sugar Pine State Park Camp Ground
Meek's Bay Resort
Camp Waisu Girl Scout Camp (West of Meek's
   Bay Resort, up Meek's Creek)
Meadow Park
Rubicon Park
D.L. Bliss State Park Campground

At the top of Rubicon Peak, hikers are inspired by the past, present, and future of the Lake of the Sky. One can envision the future of the West much as our pioneer forbearers could when they first laid eyes on the Lake. Behold the beauty of the West Shore! (SFPL.)

ABOUT THE NORTH LAKE TAHOE HISTORICAL SOCIETY

The NLTHS began in 1969 with a group of concerned residents (as so many worthy efforts do) interested in preserving Tahoe City's Gatekeeper's Cabin, which housed the gatekeeper who regulated the flow of water from Lake Tahoe into the Truckee River for decades. Since then, the NLTHS has facilitated the historically correct reconstruction of that cabin following an arson fire and converted it into a museum. In addition, the NLTHS has added the Steinbach Indian Basket Collection annex, housing more than 800 baskets from native people west of the Rocky Mountains, and it has taken over operations of the Watson Cabin Museum, a log cabin built in 1909 and located in downtown Tahoe City. The NLTHS's mission is to preserve, present, and interpret Lake Tahoe history, both regionally and in the larger context of the American West. The NLTHS, a nonprofit 501(c)(3) organization, connects visitors and locals alike with this region's lively and heady past, fostering stewardship for the lake itself and the stories of all its residents, from bears to ancient Washoe people to modern-day folks.

Please e-mail the North Lake Tahoe Historical Society at info@tahoemuseums.org to contribute to Lake Tahoe history with oral histories, family documents, letters, photographs, or ephemera. The Tahoe lifestyle, good times, wildlife, recreational opportunities, and water deserve our protection. Everyone has a part in saving this wonderful resource.

North Lake Tahoe Historical Society
P.O. Box 6141
Tahoe City, CA 96145
530.583.1762
www.northtahoemuseums.org

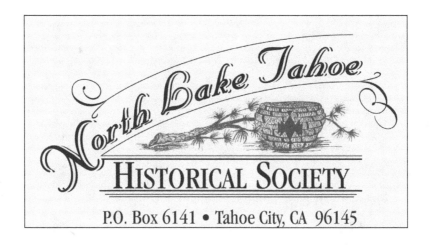

NORTH LAKE TAHOE HISTORICAL SOCIETY
P.O. Box 6141 • Tahoe City, CA 96145

Visit us at
arcadiapublishing.com

Printed in the USA
CPSIA information can be obtained
at www.ICGtesting.com
LVHW070742121223
766160LV00008B/92